Patrick Kanouse

The nook™ Book

An Unofficial Guide

SECOND EDITION

  800 East 96th Street, Indianapolis, Indiana 46240

ISBN-10: 0-7897-4908-4

ISBN-13: 978-0-7897-4908-6

The Library of Congress Cataloging-in-Publication data is on file.

Printed in the United States of America

First Printing: July 2011

Trademarks

All terms mentioned in this book that are known to be trademarks or service marks have been appropriately capitalized. Que Publishing cannot attest to the accuracy of this information. Use of a term in this book should not be regarded as affecting the validity of any trademark or service mark.

NOOK, NOOK Color, NOOK Study, NOOK for iPad, NOOK for iPhone, NOOK for Android, NOOK for PC, NOOK for Mac, NOOK Kids for iPad, NOOK Friends, LendMe, PubIt!, NOOK Kids, NOOK Book enhanced, NOOK Bookstore, NOOK Store, and all other Barnes & Noble marks in the book are trademarks of Barnes & Noble, Inc. and its affiliates.

Use of terms in this book that are trademarks of Barnes & Noble, Inc. and its affiliates does not imply any association with or endorsement by Barnes & Noble, Inc. or its affiliates, and no association or endorsement is intended or should be inferred.

Warning and Disclaimer

Every effort has been made to make this book as complete and as accurate as possible, but no warranty or fitness is implied. The information provided is on an "as is" basis. The author and the publisher shall have neither liability nor responsibility to any person or entity with respect to any loss or damages arising from the information contained in this book or from the use of the programs accompanying it.

Bulk Sales

Que Publishing offers excellent discounts on this book when ordered in quantity for bulk purchases or special sales. For more information, please contact

U.S. Corporate and Government Sales
1-800-382-3419
corpsales@pearsontechgroup.com

For sales outside of the U.S., please contact

International Sales
international@pearson.com

Editor-in-Chief
Greg Wiegand

Acquisitions Editor
Loretta Yates

Development Editor
Todd Brakke

Managing Editor
Kristy Hart

Project Editor
Betsy Harris

Copy Editor
Apostrophe Editing Services

Proofreader
Water Crest Publishing

Senior Indexer
Cheryl Lenser

Technical Editor
Todd Brakke

Publishing Coordinator
Cindy Teeters

Cover Designer
Anne Jones

Compositor
Nonie Ratcliff

Table of Contents

About the Author

Patrick Kanouse works as the structured authoring program manager for Pearson Education. Always a bookworm, he has gladly adopted ebook reading technologies, while still appreciating and valuing the printed book.

Patrick also teaches business technical report writing at IUPUI. Outside of teaching about writing, reading on his NOOK Color™, and writing about his NOOK Color, he writes poetry, publishing a PubIt™ book at BN.com that you can read on your NOOK Color or NOOK™. His website is patrickkanouse.com.

Patrick lives in Westfield, Indiana, with his wife and two Yorkies.

Dedication

This book is dedicated to my wife, Gina, who has always supported my every endeavor, even if it is immersed in some ancient history reading or volumes of poetry. Without her support, nothing that I attempt would be possible.

Acknowledgments

This book would not have been possible without Jim Cheshire's first edition, which was so well written that updating its content for this new edition was a minor task indeed. Thanks to Loretta Yates for asking me to revise and write this edition and to the efforts of the book team to make my words sound good: Todd Brakke, Betsy Harris, and San Dee Phillips.

I also appreciate the efforts of Angie Doyle, Mark Meyer, Jonathon Taylor, Beth Jonap, and John Herrin in assisting in testing the LendMe™ functions.

We Want to Hear from You!

As the reader of this book, *you* are our most important critic and commentator. We value your opinion and want to know what we're doing right, what we could do better, what areas you'd like to see us publish in, and any other words of wisdom you're willing to pass our way.

As an associate publisher for Que Publishing, I welcome your comments. You can email or write me directly to let me know what you did or didn't like about this book—as well as what we can do to make our books better.

Please note that I cannot help you with technical problems related to the topic of this book. We do have a User Services group, however, where I will forward specific technical questions related to the book.

When you write, please be sure to include this book's title and author as well as your name, email address, and phone number. I will carefully review your comments and share them with the author and editors who worked on the book.

Email: feedback@quepublishing.com

Mail: Greg Wiegand
            Associate Publisher
            Que Publishing
            800 East 96th Street
            Indianapolis, IN 46240 USA

Reader Services

Visit our website and register this book at quepublishing.com/register for convenient access to any updates, downloads, or errata that might be available for this book.

Introduction to the Second Edition

On April 25, 2011, B&N released version 1.2.0 of the NOOK Color firmware. This update adds many significant features, including

▶ NOOK Apps™ and app store

▶ NOOK Friends™

▶ Enhanced NOOK Books™ (ebooks with video, and so on)

▶ NOOK Kids™ Read and Play

▶ Full-featured email

▶ Enhanced Internet browsing with Flash support

This latest version of this book includes this additional coverage.

I was greatly assisted by Beth Jonap on Chapter 10. She helped me ensure that my instructions were correct and tested out, patiently, some ideas. However, any errors in Chapter 10 are solely mine. On May 23, 2011, B&N announced a new version of the NOOK, replacing the "original" NOOK or NOOK first edition. The new NOOK features a full-touch E Ink screen, doing away with the bottom color touchscreen and adapting a lot of the NOOK Color interface for the E Ink display. The new device is smaller, but extremely comfortable and very powerful. It's also focused primarily as an eReader, discarding the browser, Sudoku and chess games, and the music player.

Introduction

Congratulations on your purchase of the NOOK Color or NOOK, Barnes & Noble's (simply B&N from here on) ebook readers. The NOOK Color, which debuted in November 2010, is a multitouch VividView color screen. The touchscreen NOOK, which first went on sale in June 2011, features an E Ink reading display that bears a remarkable resemblance to paper.

The NOOK Color resembles a tablet like the iPad or Samsung Galaxy in many ways, but B&N has intentionally focused it as an ereading device without the full set of features to be found in a tablet. This focuses attention on the reading experience of books, newspapers, and magazines while keeping the price down. The NOOK Color is an attempt to balance the features of the tablet with the immersive experience of reading. The NOOK Color can hold approximately 6,000 books out-of-the-box. (The original NOOK can hold approximately 1,500 books.) In other words, if you read one book per week, your NOOK Color can hold enough books for almost 116 years of reading, and if you add a microSD card to your NOOK Color, you can easily hold enough books for many lifetimes!

> TIP: Many NOOK Color owners refer to other NOOK Color owners as NOOKies.

This book is intended to give you all the information you need to get the most out of your NOOK Color and the associated supporting applications. You not only learn how to use your NOOK Color and NOOK, but you also learn all the best places to get books and other content. After you've learned all the great resources available for books, you'll quickly find that you need a way to organize your ebooks, so you also learn how to do that using a free tool called Calibre.

By the time you finish this book, you'll be comfortable with all aspects of your NOOK Color and NOOK. Following are some of the many things you can learn how to do in this book:

▶ Add your own pictures for use as a wallpaper or screensaver.

▶ Use the B&N's unique LendMe feature to lend and borrow books.

▶ Play music, audiobooks, podcasts, and more.

▶ Watch video.

▶ Read your ebooks on your iPhone, iPod Touch, iPad, computer, Android phone, or Blackberry.

▶ Get books (many free) from many sources on the Internet and load them onto your NOOK Color and NOOK.

▶ Manage all your ebooks, and update author and title information if needed.

▶ Automatically download full-color covers for your books that display on your NOOK Color and NOOK.

▶ Use your NOOK Color to browse the Web.

▶ Use your NOOK Color to read enhanced books and children's books.

▶ Use highlights, annotations, and bookmarks.

▶ Learn how to publish your books using B&N's PubIt feature.

▶ Install third-party applications on your NOOK Color to add functionality to it.

This book is divided into three parts:

▶ Part I, "NOOK Color," focuses exclusively on using the NOOK Color.

▶ Part II, "NOOK," focuses on using the NOOK.

▶ Part III, "Beyond the NOOKs," focuses on using the NOOK-related apps, Calibre, and B&N's PubIt.

Mixed in with all this, you can find plenty of tips and tricks to help you get the most from your NOOK Color and NOOK. You can also find a comprehensive list of questions and answers based on questions from actual NOOK Color and NOOK owners.

> NOTE: Writing this book presents a unique challenge. The E Ink NOOK has some limitations with images. Although the images do appear, complex images or images with lots of information can be tedious to see. The NOOK Color, however, presents images in a much better fashion, as do the related NOOK Apps (excepting the Blackberry eReader app). Hence, for all aspects of the NOOK Color and NOOK Apps, the use of images will be more substantial than with the original NOOK chapters.

NOTE: Throughout this book, you will encounter the terms *ebook* and *NOOK Book*. ebook will be used generically. NOOK Books is what B&N calls its version of ebooks that it sells through B&N. These are still ebooks, and NOOK Book is more of a marketing piece, but the distinction is useful because only NOOK Books sync between devices and support social features. Also, only NOOK Books are visible in My NOOK Library on BN.com.

It's my hope that you don't have any questions about using your NOOK after reading this book, but if you do, please don't hesitate to send me email at NOOK@patrickkanouse.com. I'll gladly help if I can.

Thank you for buying *The NOOK Book*!

CHAPTER 1

Getting Started with Your NOOK Color

Before we get into the details of using your NOOK Color, let's take a look at some of the basics: gestures, setup, and basic navigation. With these basics in place, we'll then be able to discover all the other incredible things your NOOK Color can do.

> NOTE: Barnes & Noble uses a lowercase *n* when it spells *NOOK Color* and for the NOOK Color's logo.

Understanding NOOK Color Gestures

The NOOK Color, excepting the Power button, Home button, and volume controls, is controlled by gestures:

- **Tap**: This is the most common gesture. Just press your finger to the screen and raise it. Usually you use this gesture with buttons and covers.

- **Press and Hold**: This is the same as the Tap gesture, but instead of raising your finger, you hold it to the screen for a couple of seconds. This often opens an additional menu from which to choose by a Tap, but you can encounter other results from a Press and Hold.

- **Swipe Left/Swipe Right**: The gesture, mostly, for turning pages. Like a Tap, touch your finger on the screen and quickly drag it to the left (or right) and lift your finger up.

- **Scroll**: Essentially the vertical version of the Swipe gesture. You can control the speed of the scroll by swiping up or down more rapidly. You can slow down or stop the scroll by Tapping the screen (to stop) or Pressing and Holding to slow the scroll.

- **Pinch and Zoom In/Pinch and Zoom Out**: This is a method for zooming in or out on pictures, PDFs, web pages, and so on. To zoom in or show part of the screen more closely, you place your index finger and thumb closely together on the screen (that is, pinch) and spread them apart. To zoom out or show more of the screen, you do the Pinch and Zoom In gesture in reverse—this is also called Unpinch.

Setting Up and Registering Your NOOK Color

When you first turn on your NOOK Color, you see a video that walks you through the basics of getting started, though you can tap Skip This Video. (You can see the video and some others related to using the NOOK Color at http://www.barnesandnoble.com/nookcolor/support/).

The first step in getting started with your NOOK Color is to set up and register it with Barnes & Noble (simply B&N from now on). First, you need to agree to the terms of service (see Figure 1.1). Then you see a screen to set your time zone. Choose your time zone and tap Next.

FIGURE 1.1   The Terms and Conditions screen appears when you start registering your NOOK Color.

The next step is to set up the Wi-Fi access (see Figure 1.2). You can go to a B&N store, and your NOOK Color will recognize its network and log on automatically. More likely, though, you are at home, so you need to set up the NOOK Color to access your wireless network.

FIGURE 1.2   Pick your Wi-Fi network.

After you choose your time zone, your NOOK Color searches for available networks. Choose your network. If it is password protected, you will be provided the opportunity to enter a password.

> NOTE: Want Wi-Fi access on the go? The NOOK Color and NOOK Wi-Fi need only a wireless network to access the Daily (articles from B&N), subscription content, and so on. Many wireless companies such as Verizon offer mobile Wi-Fi hotspots at reasonable prices. A mobile hotspot uses the 3G or 4G cellular network but treats it as a Wi-Fi connection, so you never need to be without wireless access.

Next you register your NOOK Color. After signing on to a Wi-Fi network, you land on the Sign In screen. If you have an existing B&N account, enter your account information and tap Submit. If you don't have an account, you can create one by tapping Create an Account. Fill out the form and tap Submit (see Figure 1.3).

FIGURE 1.3 Create a B&N account if you do not already have one.

NOTE: You can also set up a B&N account on your computer by visiting www.NOOKcolor.com/setup.

For more information on connecting your NOOK Color to a Wi-Fi hotspot after your initial set up, **see** "Using Wi-Fi Hotspots," later in this chapter.

TIP: There's a great walk-through video showing how to register your NOOK Color at http://www.barnesandnoble.com/nookcolor/support/.

To register your NOOK Color, you also need to provide a default credit card with a valid billing address to be associated with your B&N account. That said, you aren't required to register your NOOK Color, but if you want to purchase ebooks from the B&N store, lend and borrow books using the LendMe feature, or use the special features available while in a B&N store, you need to register.

Using Wi-Fi Hotspots

Your NOOK Color can connect to Wi-Fi networks other than the one you initially set up. B&N offers free Wi-Fi access in all B&N stores. If you take your NOOK Color to a B&N store, it will automatically connect to the Wi-Fi hotspot in that store.

For more information on using your NOOK Color in a B&N store, **see** Chapter 9, "Shopping and Visiting B&N on Your NOOK Color."

To connect your NOOK Color to a Wi-Fi hotspot other than one in a B&N store, follow these steps:

1. Tap the Nav Arrow. (It's the up-point arrow just above the Home button.) This displays the Quick Nav Bar. You look at the Quick Nav Bar later, but for now tap Settings.

2. Tap Wireless on the touchscreen. If Wi-Fi is Off, tap Off to turn it On.

3. Tap the Wi-Fi hotspot you want to use. (Your NOOK Color displays the SSID for all Wi-Fi hotspots in range.)

4. If required, enter the password for your Wi-Fi hotspot

5. Tap Connect.

Your NOOK Color should now indicate that it is connected; you should see the Wi-Fi signal indicator in the Status Bar on the bottom right next to the battery indicator.

If your Wi-Fi hotspot isn't listed after you turn on Wi-Fi or is not in the list of Wireless Networks, tap Other Network. You can then enter the service set identifier (SSID), select the type of security (if the Wi-Fi is secured), and enter the password for your Wi-Fi hotspot if necessary. If you don't know this information, ask the person who set up the Wi-Fi network.

Your NOOK Color can connect to a Wi-Fi hotspot that requires you to browse to a web page to authenticate yourself. For example, many hotel Wi-Fi hotspots require you to enter a room number or other information to connect. You can connect to a Wi-Fi hotspot that has this requirement by launching the web browser from the Quick Nav Bar after you've joined the Wi-Fi network.

Does My NOOK Color's Battery Drain Faster with Wi-Fi Connected?

I tested my NOOK Color's battery life using Wi-Fi hotspots. In my testing, the battery life was quite a bit shorter when using Wi-Fi than when not. However, Wi-Fi affects battery life only when your NOOK Color is actually connected to a Wi-Fi hotspot. Simply having Wi-Fi turned on doesn't affect battery life.

You can significantly improve battery life by turning off Wi-Fi.

Disconnecting and Forgetting a Wi-Fi Hotspot

If you want to stop using a Wi-Fi hotspot, you have two options: disconnect or forget. Disconnect just prevents your NOOK Color from connecting to that Wi-Fi hotspot. Forgetting the hotspot removes the information about the hotspot from your NOOK Color. If you later want to reconnect to that hotspot, you will have to set it up all over again. To disconnect or forget a Wi-Fi hotspot, follow these steps:

1. Tap the Nav Arrow. This displays the Quick Nav Bar.

2. Tap Settings. This displays the Settings screen.

3. If Wi-Fi is turned off, turn it on.

4. Tap the Wi-Fi hotspot. This displays a pop-up window.

5. Tap Forget to disconnect from the Wi-Fi hotspot.

For more information on configuring the settings in your NOOK Color (including turning off the Wi-Fi card), **see** "Your NOOK Color's Settings" in Chapter 2, "Customizing and Configuring Your NOOK Color."

Caring for Your NOOK Color's Battery

Your NOOK Color uses a high-tech battery called a lithium polymer battery. Unlike older rechargeable batteries, your NOOK Color's battery doesn't suffer from a charge "memory." However, you should still follow some basic rules to maximize the life of your battery:

▶ Try to avoid fully discharging your battery. Recharge it when it gets down to about 20% or so. Although charging it repeatedly is not necessarily a bad thing, the battery seems to function optimally if you charge it only when it drops down toward that 20% area.

▶ To maximize battery life, turn off Wi-Fi and leave it off.

▶ Avoid high heat. Reading in sunlight is fine, but avoid storing your NOOK Color near a heat source.

▶ If storing your NOOK Color for a long period (a week or more), charge the battery to about 50% rather than giving it a full charge.

By following these steps, your NOOK Color's battery should last years. If you do need to replace the battery, contact B&N Customer Service.

Charging Your NOOK Color's Battery

You can charge your NOOK Color's battery either by plugging your NOOK Color into your computer's USB port or by plugging your NOOK Color into a wall outlet using the supplied AC adapter. Plugging your NOOK Color into a wall outlet charges the NOOK Color more quickly.

TIP: Just like any electronic device, your NOOK Color is susceptible to power spikes and other electrical anomalies. If you want to ensure that your NOOK Color is protected from electrical problems, plug it into a surge suppressor.

When You Are Not Reading

When you finish reading, you should let your NOOK Color go to sleep instead of turning it off. You can force the NOOK Color to sleep by pressing and quickly letting go of the Power button.

By leaving your NOOK Color on with Wi-Fi on, it will occasionally download content from B&N such as subscription content and any books that you purchase from the B&N website. When you're ready to start reading again, simply press and release the power switch at the top of your NOOK Color to wake it up. Alternatively, you can press the Home button.

Your NOOK Color's Controls

Before you get into enjoying content on your NOOK Color, let's go over the controls on your NOOK Color (see Figure 1.4).

The Power Button

The Power button is the sole button on the top left side of the NOOK Color. In addition to powering your NOOK Color on and off, the Power button can wake your NOOK Color when it's sleeping or put it to sleep when you finish reading.

To put your NOOK Color to sleep or wake it using the Power button, press and release the Power button quickly. To turn off your NOOK Color, press and hold the Power button for 5 seconds. To turn on your NOOK Color again, press and release the Power button quickly.

Power button ——

—— Volume controls

Micro SD Card
slot (on back)

∩

—— Home button

FIGURE 1.4   Your NOOK Color's controls.

The Home Button

The Home button is identified by the NOOK Color logo (a lowercase n) and is located in the center of the black bar along at the bottom of the touchscreen display. Like the Power button, the Home button performs more than one function.

You can wake your NOOK Color by pressing the Home button. If the touchscreen is already illuminated, tapping the Home button takes you to your NOOK Color's Home screen.

The Volume Buttons

These two buttons at the top right of the NOOK Color control the volume. If no videos, music, or other sounds is playing, the Volume buttons control the Notification volume (that is, when something new arrives such as subscription content). When video, music, or other sounds are playing, the Volume buttons control the sound of the media.

How Should I Clean My NOOK Color's Touchscreen?

Your NOOK Color's touchscreen is going to get dirty and covered in fingerprints. The best way to clean it is using a dry, microfiber cloth like the one you would use to clean eyeglasses. If you must use a cleaning fluid, spray it lightly on the cloth and then wipe the touchscreen. Use only cleaning sprays designed for cleaning LCD screens.

The Standard Touchscreen Menus

Because you interact with your NOOK Color almost wholly by touch, it is a good idea to become oriented to the basic, consistent menus that you will see. The basics are covered here, but as you move along through the book, the details of each menu and its offerings will be provided.

The Home Screen

The Home screen is the default opening screen (assuming you are not reading a book) and the screen you end up on if you press the Home button. The Home screen has several features (see Figure 1.5).

FIGURE 1.5   The Home screen offers many ways to open ebooks.

▶ **The Daily Shelf**: The Daily is a row of cover icons just above the Nav Arrow. You can swipe left and right through the covers. These are recently downloaded items such as today's newspaper or books purchased. You can press and hold and then drag one of the icons into the area above the Daily to keep that content readily available. You can also tap the cover to open it.

▶ **Keep Reading**: This button at the top right displays the title of the latest item you were reading. Tapping it opens that book or magazine for reading.

▶ **More**: This button at the top displays a list of recently read items, divided up into general categories: Books, Periodicals, and Files. You can tap the title to open that content for reading.

▶ **Home Page**: This is the area above the Daily and below the Keep Reading and More buttons. This is an area for you to place frequently read items or items you quickly want to access. The Home Page actually is three pages. To switch from page to page, swipe right or left.

The Quick Nav Bar

You access the Quick Nav Bar by tapping the Nav Arrow. The Quick Nav Bar provides access to many features (see Figure 1.6):

▶ **Library**: Tapping this button takes you to your library where you can access books, documents, magazines, newspapers, and more.

▶ **Shop**: Tapping this button opens the B&N bookstore, from which you can purchase content and see recommendations.

▶ **Search**: Tapping this button searches your NOOK Color for the text you enter.

▶ **Apps**: Tapping this button takes you to the NOOK Apps installed on the device.

▶ **Web**: Tapping this button takes you to the web browser.

▶ **Settings**: Tapping this button takes you to the Settings screen.

FIGURE 1.6   The Quick Nav Bar is your friend.

The Status Bar

The bar at the bottom of the touchscreen provides a plethora, depending on what you've got active or enabled on your device, of informational items along with a couple of points of quick access (from left to right):

▶ **Wireless Networks**: If wireless networks are in the area you can connect to but you are not currently connected to (assuming you have Wi-Fi on), the Wireless icon with a question mark appears. Tapping it, opens up a screen for you to connect to one of those networks.

▶ **Pandora**: If you have Pandora on, tapping this button displays the current song playing. Tapping that takes you to the Pandora app.

▶ **Email:** When new email arrives, a Mail icon appears. You can tap it to access the NOOK Color's Email app.

▶ **Music Play**: If you have Music Player on, tapping this button displays the current song playing. Tapping that takes you to the Music Player app.

▶ **Notifications**: If you tap a blank part of this screen, a notification bubble pops up letting you know about any new downloads.

▶ **Reading Now**: Tapping this button opens the current content being read (functions like the Keep Reading button at the top of the Home screen).

▶ **Nav Arrow**: Tapping this open the Quick Nav Bar.

▶ **Wi-Fi**: If you see the Wi-Fi logo, the NOOK Color is connected to a Wi-Fi hotspot.

▶ **Battery**: Provides a visual indication of the amount of charge remaining on the battery.

▶ **Time**: Provides the current time.

If you tap the area where the Wi-Fi logo and battery items are, a Quick Settings screen opens (see Figure 1.7). Besides seeing the current date and battery charge, you can turn Wi-Fi on or off, mute all sounds, enable or disable automatic orientation of the screen depending on the orientation of your NOOK Color, and adjust the brightness. (Tap Brightness and then adjust the slider by tapping and dragging.) For more information about the orientation setting, **see** the "Auto-Rotate Screen" bullet in Chapter 2.

If you need to access more settings beyond the Quick Settings, tap the Gear icon.

FIGURE 1.7   The Quick Settings screen provides quick access to several common settings.

CHAPTER 2

Customizing and Configuring Your NOOK Color

Your NOOK Color has many features that enable you to easily customize it and make it your own. There are also many settings that control how your NOOK Color operates. In this chapter, you examine how to customize and configure your NOOK Color.

Using Custom Wallpaper

You can customize your NOOK Color by using custom wallpaper images. Wallpaper appears on the Home pages when you are on the Home screen.

Choosing a Wallpaper

The easiest place to change your NOOK Color's wallpaper is to go to the Home screen. Here's how:

1. Make sure your NOOK Color is at the Home screen by pressing the Home button.

2. In an area of the Home page without a cover, press and hold. A pop-up menu appears (see Figure 2.1).

3. Tap Change Wallpaper.

4. Tap either Wallpaper or Photo Gallery (see Figure 2.2). Wallpaper are images provided by B&N or images you have loaded into the Wallpaper folder. Photo Gallery displays any photographs in JPG, PNG, or GIF formats you have placed on your NOOK Color.

5. If you chose Wallpaper, choose the wallpaper you want, and you are taken back to the Home screen with that image as the wallpaper. If you chose Photo Gallery, choose the photo you want. An enlarged version of the photo appears with an orange outlined box and two buttons: Save and Discard.

FIGURE 2.1   This menu appears when you press and hold on a blank area of the Home page.

FIGURE 2.2   Make use of B&N provided image, add your own, or browse the Photo Gallery.

TIP: You can place images you want to use for wallpaper in the Wallpaper folder on your NOOK Color. (Plug your NOOK Color into your computer and navigate to that folder.) Because the Photo Gallery displays every JPG, GIF, and PNG file on your NOOK Color, including cover images, the Photo Gallery list can quickly become lengthy.

6. The orange outlined box is for cropping the image to the size of the wallpaper (see Figure 2.3). Whatever is *inside* the orange outlined box will be used for the wallpaper. To move that box, press and hold and then drag it around to wherever you want it. Tap Save to make it the wallpaper and return to the Home screen, or tap Discard to exit to the Home screen.

FIGURE 2.3   Pick the area of the image you want to use for your Home screen.

Following is a beneficial alternative method while you are browsing your photos:

1. Tap the Nav Arrow.

2. Tap Apps.

3. Tap Gallery.

4. Tap the photo you want to make your wallpaper. This makes that photo appear on the screen.

5. Tap the photo and then tap Wallpaper in the menu options that appear at the bottom of the image.

6. The orange outlined box is for cropping the image to the size of the wallpaper. Whatever is *inside* the orange outlined box appears as the wallpaper. To move that box, press and hold and then drag it around to wherever you want it. Tap Save to make it the wallpaper and return to the Home screen, or tap Discard to exit to the photo.

Should You Use a Specific File Format for Images?

Your NOOK Color supports JPEG, GIF, and PNG files. For images, using either JPEG or PNG is your best option. GIF isn't a good option for photographs, but if your image is a line art or text, GIF can work fine. If you're unsure, stick with JPEG.

One Step Further—Decals

If you want to take the ultimate step in customizing your NOOK Color, a DecalGirl skin (www.decalgirl.com) is the perfect addition. DecalGirl skins are vinyl skins with adhesive backing that you can easily apply. Many skins also include matching NOOK Color wallpaper that provides a truly unique look.

Your NOOK Color's Settings

Your NOOK Color offers configurable settings for controlling many of its features. Tap Settings on the Quick Nav Bar to access the Settings screen (see Figure 2.4).

Device Info Menu

The Device Info menu shown in Figure 2.5 displays battery charge, available storage on the NOOK Color, microSD card storage, information about your NOOK Color, legal information, and a way to deregister the device. For more information on adding a microSD card to your NOOK Color, see "Adding and Using a microSD Card to Your NOOK Color." This screen also displays your NOOK Color's serial number along with your NOOK Color's MAC address—the hardware address of the Wi-Fi modem.

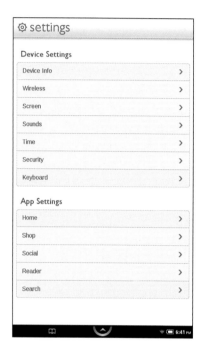

FIGURE 2.4 The Settings screen contains many options.

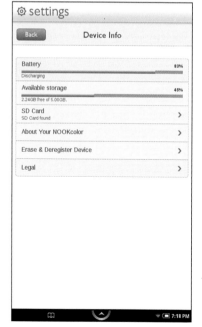

FIGURE 2.5 The Device Info menu.

If you tap About Your NOOK Color, you see your profile information: owner name, account ID, and so on. Here you can see the software version (called *firmware*) currently installed on your NOOK Color. B&N releases periodic updates to the NOOK Color to improve performance and fix known issues. As long as your NOOK Color has a connection to a Wi-Fi connection, your NOOK Color can automatically download any updates that B&N releases.

Not all NOOK Color owners receive new firmware updates at the same time. B&N rolls out new firmware over a period of about a week. If you want to manually update your NOOK Color, you can visit www.barnesandnoble.com/NOOKcolor/support where B&N typically provides instructions for manually updating your NOOK Color to the latest firmware.

If you tap Erase & Deregister, you will be warned that doing so removes all books and files, including sideloaded content, and deregistering the device. Then you have a button to do just that. You should not do this except for potentially severe problems with the NOOK Color. More likely, you will use this if you are done with the NOOK Color and want to give it to a friend.

> NOTE: Sideloaded content refers to all the ebooks from sources other than B&N and files you have placed on your NOOK Color. The action of putting these files and ebooks on the NOOK Color is called *sideloading*.

The Legal option provides more options to review the terms and conditions and such.

Wireless Menu

The Wireless menu provides options to turn the Wi-Fi on or off and to connect to Wi-Fi hotspots, which you have already done during the setup process in Chapter 1, "Getting Started with Your NOOK Color," in the "Using Wi-Fi Hotspots" section.

Screen Menu

The Screen menu contains several options for configuring your NOOK Color's display (see Figure 2.6):

  ▶ **Auto-Rotate Screen**: This setting, on by default, enables switching from portrait to landscape mode automatically. Your NOOK Color has an accelerometer in it that senses whether you hold the NOOK Color upright or on its side. Much content can be viewed in either fashion (though not all). If you are reading or viewing content that can be in either, whenever you change from portrait to landscape or vice versa, the content adjusts its orientation as well.

FIGURE 2.6   The Screen menu.

NOTE: Some content, for example children's ebooks, are set up for either portrait or landscape mode but not both. Turning off automatic orientation does not
alter this. Therefore, if you have automatic orientation off, hold the NOOK Color
in portrait mode, and open a children's ebook, that ebook appears in landscape
mode.

▶ **Brightness**: This setting controls the maximum brightness of the screen. To
   adjust the brightness, tap Brightness, and then drag your finger to adjust the
   slider (see Figure 2.7). When you are happy with the setting, tap OK to
   return to the menu.

▶ **Screen Timeout**: This controls the time interval after which your NOOK
   Color puts itself to sleep. This timer is set to 2 minutes by default. To change
   the interval, tap Screen Timeout, and then tap the preferred time interval.

TIP: If you set the sleep timer to a time interval that is shorter than the
amount of time it takes you to read a page on the reading screen, your NOOK
Color goes into sleep mode while you are reading. So, be sure you set the interval appropriately for your reading speed.

FIGURE 2.7   Adjusting the brightness of your screen lower at night makes for easier reading.

Sounds Menu

The Sounds menu contains several options for configuring your NOOK Color's sound settings (see Figure 2.8):

▶ **Mute**: This setting turns off all sound. Even though it says "except for media," it mutes everything.

▶ **Media**: This setting adjusts the volume for music, videos, and other media sound such as the reading segments of children's ebooks. To adjust the volume, tap Media Volume, and then drag your finger to adjust the slider. When you are happy with the setting, tap OK to return to the menu.

▶ **Notification Volume**: This setting adjusts the volume for notifications such as disconnecting the NOOK Color from your computer. To adjust the volume, tap Notification Volume, and then drag your finger to adjust the slider. When you are happy with the setting, tap OK to return to the menu.

FIGURE 2.8   The Sounds menu.

Time Menu

The Time menu contains several options for configuring your NOOK Color's time settings (see Figure 2.9):

▶ **Use 24-Hour Format**: This enables you to choose between a 12-hour time format and a 24-hour time format.

▶ **Select Time Zone**: This setting enables you to select your current local time zone. Your NOOK Color normally gets the current time using Wi-Fi access. However, if Wi-Fi service isn't available, it still displays the current time, provided you have configured your time zone. If you do not see the time zone you need here, tap Show All World Time Zones to see a longer list.

FIGURE 2.9   The Time menu.

Security Menu

The Security menu contains several options for configuring your NOOK Color's security settings (see Figure 2.10):

- ▶ **Change Unlock Passcode**: This enables you to choose a four-digit passcode (or PIN) to lock your NOOK Color when it goes to sleep or powers off (see Figure 2.11). Changing the passcode requires entering the soon-to-be-old passcode. (The first time you open this menu, you may see Set Unlock Passcode instead of Change Unlock Passcode.)

- ▶ **Require Passcode**: This setting enables the use of a passcode or not when the NOOK Color powers on or is awoken from sleep. To gain access to the content on the NOOK Color, a person must correctly enter the passcode.

NOTE: Forgot your passcode? The good news is that you can get your NOOK Color back. The bad news is that you have to reset your NOOK Color to factory settings, which means you lose all content you placed on your device.

To reset your NOOK Color to factory settings:

1. With the NOOK Color off, hold the Home button and the Power button.

2. The NOOK Color starts up. Keep holding the buttons.

3. After a few seconds, you see a screen to reset your NOOK Color to factory settings with two options:

   ▶ Press Power to exit.

   ▶ Press Home to continue.

4. Press the Home button. You see the two options again.

5. Press the Home button.

6. Your NOOK Color erases the data, deregisters, and reboots the device.

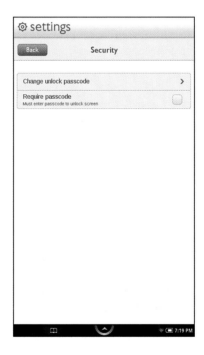

FIGURE 2.10 The Security menu.

FIGURE 2.11   The passcode is a PIN for your NOOK Color.

Keyboard Menu

The Keyboard menu contains several options for configuring your NOOK Color's keyboard settings (see Figure 2.12):

▶ **Keyboard Sounds**: This enables you to set whether, when you type on the virtual keyboard, you hear click sounds every time you tap a key.

▶ **Auto-Capitalization**: This setting enables the NOOK Color to auto-capitalize while typing. For example, if you type a period, for the next letter you type, the NOOK Color capitalizes it. (If you don't want to capitalize that letter, tap the Shift key, which enables you to enter a lowercase letter.)

▶ **Quick Fixes**: This setting enables the NOOK Color to correct common misspellings. For example, if you type "teh," the NOOK Color automatically changes that to "the."

FIGURE 2.12   The Keyboard menu.

Home Menu

The Home menu contains several options for configuring your NOOK Color's Home Screen settings (see Figure 2.13).

In the General Home Settings section:

- ▶ **Set Wallpaper**: This enables you to set the wallpaper. For more information about setting your wallpaper, **see** "Choosing a Wallpaper."

- ▶ **Clear Keep Reading List**: This setting enables you to clear the Keep Reading and More lists. The lists starts anew as you read content.

- ▶ **Clear Daily Shelf**: This setting enables you to clear the daily shelf of items.

In the Daily Shelf Items section, you have a few more specific controls about what appears on the Daily Shelf. Each of the items enables you to select whether you want to see such items on the Daily Shelf. For Recent Issues of Each Newspaper and Magazine settings, tap the down-arrow button to see a list of options for how many issues you want to appear on the Daily Shelf. (The default is one.)

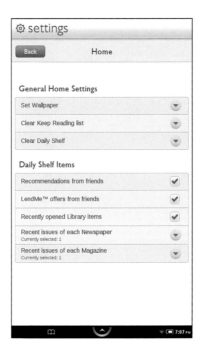

FIGURE 2.13   The Home Settings menu.

Shop Menu

The Shop menu contains several options for configuring your NOOK Color's Shop settings (see Figure 2.14):

▶ **Require Password for Purchases**: This enables you to require a password entry for every purchase made through the B&N Bookstore on the NOOK Color. Leaving this option disabled means that when you click Buy in the bookstore, you purchase it without having to enter the password.

▶ **Clear Shop Recent Searches**: This setting enables you to clear the Shop Searches. Whenever you search the B&N Bookstore on the NOOK Color, it saves the recent searches. The searches are saved to make it easier to conduct searches. For example, you can search for ebooks related to Sherlock Holmes but decide not to purchase now. When you go back to the B&N Bookstore on your NOOK Color, you can type Sher, and Sherlock Holmes appears below the search text. You can then tap Sherlock Holmes and the search is performed.

FIGURE 2.14 The Shop menu.

Social Menu

The Social menu contains several options for configuring your NOOK Color's Social settings (see Figure 2.15). Basically, you can link your Facebook and Twitter accounts and Google Contacts lists to this NOOK Color, which enables you to share quotes and recommendations directly to your and your friends' Facebook walls and Twitter account.

▶ **Facebook**: This enables you to link your Facebook account to your NOOK Color. If you have already linked your Facebook account, you can unlink it. To link it, tap Link Your Account. Then enter the required information and tap Log In (see Figure 2.16). For more information about Facebook with your NOOK Color, **see** Chapter 8, "Using the Social Features of Your NOOK Color."

FIGURE 2.15 Connect your Facebook, Twitter, and Google Contacts with your NOOK Color here.

FIGURE 2.16 Link your Facebook account to your NOOK Color.

▶ **Twitter**: This enables you to link your Twitter account to your NOOK Color. If you have already linked your Twitter account, you can unlink it. To link it, tap Link Your Account. Then enter the required information and tap Sign In. Twitter asks you to allow this linking to occur. Tap Allow to do so (see Figure 2.17). For more information about Twitter with your NOOK Color, **see** Chapter 8.

FIGURE 2.17   Link your Twitter account to your NOOK Color.

▶ **Google Contacts**: This enables you to link your Google Contacts list to this NOOK Color. If you have already linked your Google Contacts list, you can unlink it. To link it, tap Link Your Account. Then enter the required information. If you want the NOOK Color to remember this information should you come back to this screen, tap the Remember Me check box; then Tap Sign In. Google wants to know if you want to grant access to the NOOK Color to do this linking. Tap Grant Access to do so (see Figure 2.18).

FIGURE 2.18   Link your Google Contacts account to your NOOK Color.

Reader Menu

The Reader menu has one option: Animate eBook Page Turns. This is off by default. Tap the check box to turn it on.

The default behavior when you tap to change a page in an ebook is for the text on the screen to simply disappear and be replaced by the next page of text. With Animate eBook Page Turns on, however, when you tap to change a page in an ebook, you see the text on that page slide either left or right and the next page of text slide into view.

Search Menu

The Search menu contains several options for configuring your NOOK Color's Search setting:

▶ **Searchable Items**: This enables you to adjust what searches are conducted on (see Figure 2.19). When you tap Search from the Quick Nav Bar, you can search a variety of different categories. By default, Apps, Browser, Music, Library, and Shop are searched. You can turn off searching on Apps, Browser, and Music.

▶ **Clear Search Shortcuts**: This setting enables you to clear the list of recent searches. Whenever you search your NOOK Color, it saves the recent searches. The searches are saved to make it easier to conduct searches.

Adding and Using a microSD Card to Your NOOK Color

Your NOOK Color has approximately 8GB of built-in memory, though B&N reserves 3GB for the operating system and other NOOK Color items—leaving 5GB of memory for your use. That's enough memory for an enormous library of books. However, it might not be enough memory if you add pictures, music, videos, and audiobooks to your NOOK Color. Therefore, your NOOK Color's memory is expandable using a microSD card.

> CAUTION: Some NOOK Color users have reported seeing only 1 GB or 5 GB of memory as the total memory when looking at the Settings for memory. I can tell you that this does not mean you have a smaller amount of memory on your device.
>
> What it does mean is that B&N is giving you less space for videos, photos, and sideloaded content in general. Some of the latest devices reserve 7 GB for the NOOK Color operating system and B&N content (NOOK Books, magazines, apps, etc.). So when users see 1 GB total memory, they are seeing the amount of space they have for non-B&N content.

FIGURE 2.19   Adjust search functions on your NOOK Color.

TIP: A microSD card is not the same as an SD memory card like the kind typically used in digital cameras. A microSD card is approximately the size of your fingernail.

NOTE: You will see both microSD and microSDHC. Your NOOK Color can use either format—they are the same. The HC is used for microSD cards greater than 2GB in size.

Installing a microSD card in your NOOK Color is easy—you don't even need to turn off your NOOK Color:

1. Flip your NOOK Color over so that the speaker is at the bottom. On the bottom right, flip up the metal plate (it's kept in place by a couple of small magnets) and pull it so that the small plastic connectors keeping the plate attached to the NOOK Color are fully extended.

2. The microSD slot is the small opening. With the metal connectors of the microSD card facing the front of the NOOK Color, slide the microSD card in, and push until it locks into place. The NOOK Color automatically recognizes the card, and you hear a beep. Close the metal plate.

3. If the microSD card has not yet been formatted, a screen appears letting you know that formatting it will erase everything on the disk. Tap Format Now. Tap Format Now again to confirm.

On the Device Info screen (from the Quick Nav Bar, tap Setting, and then tap Device Info), tap SD Card (only available to tap if a microSD card is installed). This opens the SD Card screen. Here, you can see information related to the amount of free memory available on the microSD card.

If you tap Format SD Card, you can format the microSD card, which erases everything on the card. (This option is only available after tapping Unmount SD Card.) A confirmation screen to format and erase all data on the micro SD card appears. Tap Format to do so. Tap OK when done.

1. From the SD Card screen, tap Unmount SD Card (see Figure 2.20).

FIGURE 2.20   The SD Card menu where you can safely dismount the card before removing it from your NOOK Color.

2. Flip your NOOK Color over so that the speaker is at the bottom. On the bottom right, flip up the metal plate (it's kept in place by a couple of small magnets) and pull it so that the small plastic connectors keeping the plate attached to the NOOK Color are fully extended.

3. With your finger, push the microSD card further into the slot. The microSD card partially pops out, letting you get a grip on it to pull it out completely. Close the metal plate.

When you connect your NOOK Color to your computer, you now see your microSD card in addition to your NOOK Color's built-in memory. (It is the drive called NO NAME.)

> NOTE: You can add a microSD card that already has items loaded on it, but the NOOK Color folder structure is necessary, so it is easiest to install a blank microSD card into the NOOK Color and then plug the NOOK Color into your computer and load files into the appropriate categories (documents, videos, and so on).

Now that you have a microSD card installed, how do you access those files? From the Quick Nav Bar, tap Library and then tap My Files. You see two options near the top that you do not see if you do not have a microSD card installed: My NOOK Color and Memory Card. By default, you are looking at the My NOOK Color files. Tap Memory Card to switch to seeing the files on the microSD card. (Tap My NOOK Color to go back to the NOOK Color files.) You can then tap the folders and such just as if you were working with the My Files category. (For basic instructions in interacting with these files, **see** "Reading Microsoft Office and Other Documents on Your NOOK Color" in Chapter 3, "Reading on Your NOOK Color and Beyond.")

CHAPTER 3

Reading on Your NOOK Color and Beyond

Although your NOOK Color has many unique features and capabilities, its primary purpose is for reading ebooks and other content. One of the benefits of owning a NOOK Color is that you can carry a complete library with you everywhere you go. If you don't happen to have your NOOK Color with you, you can also read your ebooks on your PC, Mac, iPhone, iPad, iPod touch, Android phone, and Blackberry.

Various forms of content are available to read on your NOOK Color—NOOK Books and other EPUB files, along with PDFs; Microsoft Word, Excel, and PowerPoint files; and plain text files. Appendix A, "Understanding ebook Formats," explains more about the details of ebook formats. You are probably already familiar with Microsoft documents, though you can use either the DOC or DOCX formats (and the corresponding XLS or XLSX and PPT or PPTX formats) used in all versions of Word.

Browsing Your Library

The two main places for content on your NOOK Color are Home screen and Library.

The Home Screen

The Home screen includes the Daily Shelf, covers you have placed on the Home pages, and other ways to access your content. (**See** the section "The Home Screen" in Chapter 1, "Getting Started with Your NOOK Color," for a complete review of the options.)

The Daily Shelf shows the most recent downloads on the left with less recent downloads on the right. Swipe left or right to see more of the Daily Shelf.

To open an ebook, magazine, or newspaper from the Home screen, tap the cover. The ebook, magazine, or newspaper opens to the last page that you were on when you closed it. However, NOOK Kids books always open from the beginning.

> TIP: On an open space of the Home page, double-tap to have the book, maga-zine, and newspaper icons align in a grid format. Alternatively, press and hold on a blank area of the screen, and then tap Clean Up This Panel to achieve the same result.

The Home screen has three Home pages. (You can see which page you are on at the top, just beneath the Keep Reading bar by the three dots—the white one is the Home page you are on.) You can add icons to the Home pages (not the Daily Shelf) by tap-ping and dragging a cover from the Daily Shelf. In the Library, you can press and hold a cover and then tap Add to Home from the menu that appears.

> NOTE: With the firmware 1.2.0 release (April 25, 2011), you can now add any books or apps to the Home screen. You are no longer limited to just adding NOOK Books to the Home screen.

To remove an item from a Home page, press and hold the cover. Tap Remove from Home from the menu that appears.

To place an item on a different Home page, press and drag the cover over to the far right or left edge of the screen. The cover will slide to the next page. Release the cover.

> NOTE: If you have difficulty moving the last cover from a Home page to another, the best way to do that is to drag the cover down to the Daily Shelf, swipe to the Home page you want it on, and then drag it from the Daily Shelf to the Home page.

Finally, you can remove an item from the Daily Shelf by pressing and holding the cover. Tap Remove from Home from the menu that appears.

The Library

The Library contains all the content you've purchased from B&N and the content you have sideloaded (see Figure 3.1). This includes not only ebooks you've purchased, but also magazine and newspaper subscriptions, sample books, videos, music, Microsoft documents, PDFs, ebooks purchased from other sources, and free books downloaded from B&N and other sites.

To go to the Library, tap Library on the Quick Nav Bar. When at the Library, a set of buttons to choose from are always available:

▶ **Books**: Tapping this displays the full list of ebooks on your NOOK Color, whether from B&N or other sources.

▶ **Magazines**: Tapping this displays the full list of magazines on your NOOK Color, whether from B&N or other sources.

▶ **Newspapers**: Tapping this displays the full list of newspapers on your NOOK Color, whether from B&N or other sources.

▶ **My Shelves**: Tapping this displays the shelves you have created and one default shelf: Archived.

▶ **My Files**: Tapping this displays the folders on your NOOK Color and microSD card if installed.

▶ **LendMe**: Tapping this displays available ebooks from your library to lend, what ebooks you have borrowed, and what ebooks you have lent. For more information on the LendMe feature, **see** Chapter 4, "Lending and Borrowing Books with LendMe on Your NOOK Color."

FIGURE 3.1 The Library where all your books and content are stored.

> NOTE: For more information on using My NOOK Library on bn.com, **see** Chapter 20, "Using My NOOK Library."

If you purchase a book using the Shop on your NOOK Color, that book is automatically downloaded to your NOOK Color within a few minutes. If you purchase an ebook from B&N using your computer, the ebook is added to My NOOK Library on bn.com, but it isn't downloaded to your NOOK Color automatically—though the cover appears. You can tell it was *not* downloaded because a green Download icon appears on the bottom of the cover. Tap the cover to download the NOOK Book.

> CAUTION: If you plan to be away from Wi-Fi hotspots, you should make sure that the items that appear in My NOOK Library have actually been downloaded to your NOOK Color.

So many options exist here, so work your way through each button and the myriad actions you can take in interacting with the Library.

Books

This is the default location after you tap Library from the Quick Nav Bar, unless you have tapped Newspapers or one of the other buttons, and then tapping Library from the Quick Nav Bar takes you to the last button you were on (see Figure 3.2). Note that all files placed in the microSD card's My Files\Books folder are shown here along with all NOOK Books and documents in the NOOK Color's My Files\Books folder or NOOK Color's Digital Editions folder.

At the top of the screen, you have the Sort and View buttons. Tapping the Sort button enables you sort your ebooks by Title, Author, or Most Recent, which means either read or added (see Figure 3.2). The View by default is Grid view. Scroll up or down to view the library. The Grid view option is a series of nine squares (see Figure 3.3). Below that, you have Shelf view (you swipe left or right to view the entire shelf), Large List view, and Small List view. You can work with various Sorts and Views. For example, if you have 10 novels by Donna Leon and you sort by Author and view by Shelf view, all of Donna Leon's books appear on a shelf. Large List view shows a medium size cover, the full title, and the author. Small list view does the same, but with a small cover.

In general, sorting by title and using Shelf view is impractical (it's essentially a Large List view) because most titles are different. Table 3.1 shows some useful combinations.

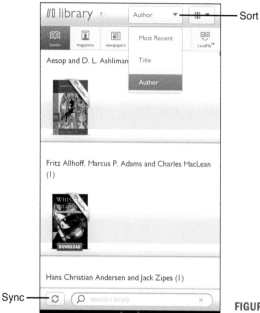

FIGURE 3.2 Sort your library by one of these choices.

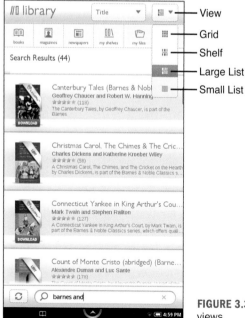

FIGURE 3.3 View your library in one of these views.

TABLE 3.1 Recommended Sort and View Combinations

Sort	View	Comments
Most Recent	Shelf	Shows the ebooks in Today, Yesterday, and date shelves
Author	Shelf	Shows the ebooks in shelves by author
Title	Grid	Shows the ebooks with large covers in a scrollable grid format
Title	Large/Small List	Shows the ebooks with covers and author information in a scrollable list format

From the Books part of the Library, you can interact with your ebooks in two ways. First, you can just tap the cover to open the ebook. Second, if you tap and hold the cover, a pop-up menu appears (see Figure 3.4) with several options:

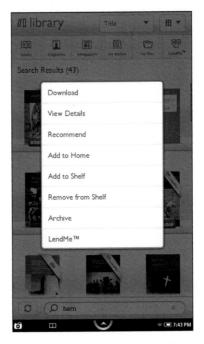

FIGURE 3.4   The pop-up menu that appears after pressing and holding a cover.

▶ **Read**: This option is only available if you have downloaded the NOOK Book. Tapping this option opens the ebook for reading.

▶ **Download**: This option is only available if you have not yet downloaded the NOOK Book. Tapping this option downloads the NOOK Book assuming you have a Wi-Fi connection enabled.

▶ **View Details**: Tapping this option opens a screen with several options (see Figure 3.5). If it is a NOOK Book, you see the star rating from B&N. Tapping the Read button opens the ebook for reading. (Alternatively, if you have not downloaded the NOOK Book yet, you can tap Download to download the NOOK Book.)

Tap LendMe to see the LendMe screen. For more information on the LendMe feature, **see** Chapter 4.

Tap Recommend It to see the Recommend screen. For more information on the Recommend feature, **see** Chapter 8, "Using the Social Features of Your NOOK Color."

The Overview tab provides text describing the ebook.

The More Like This tab provides cover images to NOOK Books that B&N's computers think are like the particular book you are viewing. Tapping one of those covers opens a View Details screen for that NOOK Book.

If the NOOK Book is a sample or borrowed (for more information related to shopping and sampling NOOK Books, **see** Chapter 9, "Shopping and Visiting B&N on Your NOOK Color." You can tap Read Sample (or just Read for borrowed NOOK Books) to read the sample or tap the Price button and then tap Confirm to purchase the NOOK Book.

▶ **Full Version Available**: This option appears for NOOK Book samples. Tapping it takes you to the View Details screen.

▶ **Recommend**: Just like Recommend It from the View Details screen, you can recommend an ebook. For more information on the Recommend feature, **see** Chapter 8.

▶ **Add to Home**: This option lets you add it to the Home page with a single tap.

▶ **Add to Shelf**: This option lets you add it to a shelf. An Add to Shelf screen appears. You can tap an existing shelf to add that ebook to that shelf. Alternatively, you can tap Add to a New Shelf. The Create New Shelf screen appears. Type in the shelf name and tap Save. The shelf is created and that ebook is added to that shelf. You can add ebooks to multiple shelves.

▶ **Remove from Shelf**: This option lets you remove the ebook from a shelf. If you tap Remove from Shelf, the Select Self screen appears and displays all the shelves this ebook is in. Tap the shelf you want to remove this ebook from.

A Sample Book's
View Details screen

Standard View
Details screen

FIGURE 3.5   The View Details screen.

▶ **Archive**: This option lets you archive a NOOK Book. This removes it from ready access, though it does not remove it from your My NOOK Library at B&N. If the NOOK Book is already archived, this option reads Unarchive. Tapping it unarchives the NOOK Book.

> TIP: You can manage your ebook library (including archiving and unarchiving items) using My NOOK Library at bn.com. My NOOK Library is covered in detail in Chapter 20.

▶ **LendMe**: As in the View Details screen, you can lend a NOOK Book from this menu. For more information on the LendMe feature, **see** Chapter 4.

Books, magazines, and newspapers purchased from B&N often have notices on the cover regarding them:

▶ **New**: This is a recent NOOK Book you have purchased and not yet downloaded.

▶ **LendMe**: This NOOK Book can be lent to a friend.

▶ **Borrowed**: You have borrowed this NOOK Book from a friend. The number of days left (out of 14) is in a small, gray circle at the bottom right of the cover.

▶ **Lent**: You have lent this NOOK Book to a friend. The number of days left (out of 14) is in a small, gray circle at the bottom right of the cover.

▶ **Sample**: This is only a portion of the NOOK Book to give you a chance to review before you buy.

▶ **Download**: The NOOK Book is not yet downloaded. Tap the cover to download it.

Magazines

This is where B&N places all your magazines (as opposed to newspapers) that you purchase from B&N (see Figure 3.6). Also, if you placed any files in either the NOOK Color's Magazines folder or in the microSD card's My Files\Magazines folder, those documents are shown here as well. You have the same options here as you do with the Books section.

FIGURE 3.6   The Magazines screen.

Newspapers

This is where B&N places all your newspapers (as opposed to magazines) that you purchase from B&N (see Figure 3.7). Also, if you have placed any files in either the NOOK Color's Newspapers folder or in the microSD card's My Files\Newspapers folder, those documents are shown here as well. You have the same options here as you do with the Books section.

My Shelves

The NOOK Color enables you to organize your ebooks into categories, or shelves, that you can name (see Figure 3.8). If you have a lot of ebooks and you want to categorize them beyond just author name, title, and most recent, this is how you can do it.

My Shelves shows you any existing shelves. (Two exist by default: Favorites and Archived.) To add a shelf, tap Create New Shelf. The Create New Shelf screen appears. Type the name of the shelf and tap Save.

FIGURE 3.7   The Newspapers screen.

FIGURE 3.8   The My Shelves view.

You can also edit existing shelves by tapping Edit next to the shelf you want to edit (see Figure 3.9). Here you can do several things. A listing of titles appears. To add titles to this shelf, tap the check box next to the title so that a check mark appears. Tap Save to add those titles to the shelf. Tapping Remove, instead, removes those titles from the shelf. Tap Rename to rename the shelf.

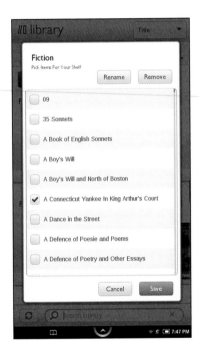

FIGURE 3.9   Edit existing shelves.

My Files

My Files lets you access files on the NOOK Color internal memory or on the microSD card. The view defaults to the files on your NOOK Color. Tap Memory Card, which appears only if a microSD card is installed, to access the files there.

The folder structure on the NOOK Color and on the microSD card is straightforward, as shown in Figure 3.10. You can view either the folders and files with small or large folder icons by tapping the View icon. Books, Magazines, and Newspapers have already been covered because they appear in the appropriate locations in the Library.

> NOTE: Adobe Digital Editions (ADE) ebooks also appear in the Books section of the Library. For more information about ADE ebooks, see Appendix A.

FIGURE 3.10   Two views of the My Shelves screen.

Interacting with documents, music, and videos is covered in the appropriate sections throughout this book.

LendMe

For more information on the LendMe feature, **see** Chapter 4.

The Sync button forces a sync with My NOOK Library, downloading any new content, and so on. You can also tap the Search Library box to search your library for particular books and such.

How Can I Delete Sideloaded Content Because There Isn't a Menu Option for Removing It?

Sideloaded content—ebooks and documents not purchased from BN.com—must be deleted by connecting your NOOK Color to your computer and removing the content. The easiest way to manage your sideloaded content is to use Calibre, a free ebook management application. Calibre is covered in Chapter 19, "Managing Your ebooks with Calibre."

Reading NOOK Books on Your NOOK Color

If you open a NOOK Book or sideloaded EPUB file for the first time, after you select it, you are taken to the starting point that the publisher has chosen for that item. This might or might not be the first page. For example, some ebooks open on the first page of Chapter 1. Other ebooks open on the cover or title page. The publisher of the book decides which page is visible when you first open an ebook.

If you are opening a NOOK Book that you have read on the NOOK Color before in any of the NOOK Apps, NOOK Study™, or original NOOK, you are taken to the last location you were reading. If you open a sideloaded EPUB file you have read on the NOOK Color before, it opens to the last page you were on in the NOOK Color. In other words, non-B&N content does not sync across applications.

As you're reading, swipe right across the page to go to the previous page or swipe left across the page to go to the next page.

Of course, there's more to reading books than just reading, right? Figure 3.11 shows the reading screen and the Reading Tools available. To see the Reading Tools, quickly tap the reading screen.

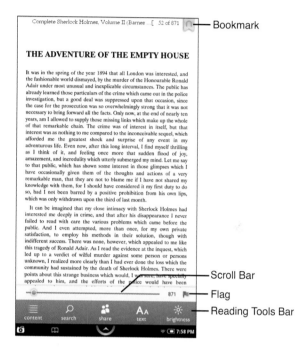

FIGURE 3.11   The reading interface.

Following are features of the Reading Tools:

▶ **Bookmark**: Tap this to add a bookmark. Chapter 5, "Using Highlights, Bookmarks, and Annotations," covers using bookmarks in detail.

▶ **Scroll Bar**: Drag this to quickly slide through the book.

▶ **Flag**: Appears only for B&N purchased content. Tap this to access some options not on the Reading Tools bar. **See** Chapter 8 for more details.

▶ **Reading Tools Bar**: This bar has five buttons: Content, Search, Share, Text, and Brightness. You see each of these buttons in action in the following sections.

To exit the Reading Tools, tap anywhere on the reading screen without those tools appearing.

Finally, while reading, you can press and hold on a word. The Text Selection Toolbar appears (see Figure 3.12). If you want to select more than that single word, drag the selection highlight to the end of the block of text you want to select. For the Highlight, Note, and Look Up button, **see** Chapter 5. For the Share button, **see** Chapter 8. Looking up words is discussed in the "Looking Up Words" section of this chapter.

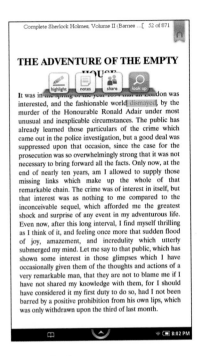

FIGURE 3.12   The Text Selection Toolbar.

Changing the Text Font and Text Size

Your NOOK Color enables you to easily change the text font and text size while reading. To change the font or the text size, tap the reading screen, and then tap Text on the Reading Tools bar (see Figure 3.13).

Your NOOK Color supports six text sizes, represented by the A. The current text size A is colored teal. Tap the A for the size you want. You can see the text size adjust behind the text menu. Adjust the text size to whichever size you want.

To change the text font, tap the Font selection, which enlarges and shows a check mark next to the current font. You have six fonts to choose from, and you can see a representation of them in the Font selection. (Scroll to see all the fonts.) You can see the font change.

- ▶ You cannot change the text font if the publisher created the content with a specific font embedded in it.

- ▶ You cannot change the text font for PDF files. If the creator of the PDF file embedded a particular font, your NOOK Color uses that font. Otherwise, it uses the default font.

▶ Some ebooks consist of pages scanned as images, usually as PDF files. You cannot change the text font for these ebooks.

FIGURE 3.13   Use this screen to adjust the font size among other things.

NOTE: Tapping Publisher Defaults to On changes all settings on this screen to the options chosen by the Publisher for all content that you read. You can toggle that back to Off at anytime.

Changing the Color Theme, Line Spacing, Margins, and Brightness

Your NOOK Color enables you to change the color scheme, space between lines, and margins while reading. To change these, tap the reading screen, and then tap Text on the Reading Tools bar.

Tap the Theme box to change the color settings for the background and text. You have six options ranging from Normal (black on white) to Night (white on black). Tap your choice. The reading screen changes to reflect that, so choose any you like.

> TIP: With Butter, the background screen is not so white. However, if you read at night with no ambient light, you might prefer the Night or Gray option.

The Line Spacing options are similar to using single-space or double-space. The current selection is in a teal color, and you have three options. Tap the option you want. The reading screen adjusts.

The Margin options determine the amount of white space on the right and left sides of the text. The current selection is in a teal color, and you have three options. Tap the option you want. The reading screen adjusts.

To adjust the Brightness of the screen, tap Brightness. You see the familiar scrollbar that you can tap and drag to the desired brightness.

Looking Up Words

One of the most convenient features of your NOOK Color is to quickly look up the definitions of words you don't know. If you're reading a book and encounter a word you don't know or are curious about, press and hold on that word until the Text Selection toolbar appears. Tap Look Up. A window appears with a dictionary entry (see Figure 3.14). You can also tap Wikipedia or Google. Tapping either takes you to the browser, opens up the corresponding website, and enters that word as the search criteria. (Tap the Keep Reading link Status bar to return quickly to your book.)

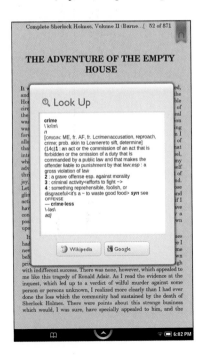

FIGURE 3.14 Your dictionary goes wherever your NOOK Color goes.

NOTE: Looking up words is not supported for certain types of ebooks:

▶ Magazines

▶ ADE PDFs and PDFs

▶ NOOK Books for Kids

To search your ebook, tap the Search button, and then type the text you want to search. A keyboard and text entry box appear. Type your search words and tap Search. If it finds your word, your NOOK Color displays the locations of that word in a scrollable window (see Figure 3.15). The scrollable window provides a bit of context. Tap the location of the word you want to go to. You are taken to that location, the word is highlighted, the scrollable window disappears, but you still see the search text box. You can tap the bottom left button to re-display the scrollable window, or you can tap the left or right keys next to the search word to go to and highlight the next appearance of that word. Tap the X or tap the reading screen to exit search mode. If you want to search for a different word or phrase, tap in the box that contains your original search term.

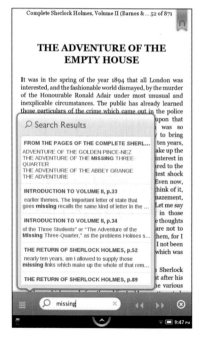

FIGURE 3.15   Searching your ebook is easy.

> TIP: Typing lots of uppercase letters? Tap the Shift key twice. (It has a white highlight around the key.) This enables you to enter only uppercase letters. Tap the Shift key again to release the caps lock.

Reading Enhanced NOOK Books

With version 1.2.0 firmware release, B&N introduced enhanced NOOK Books. Enhanced NOOK Books feature video and audio directly within the ebook. When shopping for these ebooks at BN.com, look for the NOOK Book enhanced™ designation. The cover of the NOOK Book also has a tag with video or audio showing.

When reading one of these enhanced NOOK Books, you will encounter the enhanced material, as shown in Figure 3.16.

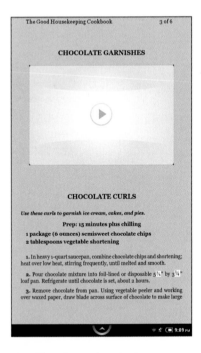

FIGURE 3.16   Here's a page with enhanced content.

Tap the Play button on the content. Tap the Play button to pause the video, and tap the Pause button to restart the video. Use the scrollbar to scroll to a specific location. Tap the Expand button (four arrows pointing away from each other) to make the video full screen.

NOTE: You cannot sample enhanced NOOK Books from B&N.

NOTE: Enhanced NOOK Books at this time work *only* on your NOOK Color. If you own a regular NOOK, you will see it listed in the Everything Else list, but you will not be able to download it. On the NOOK App for iPad, you will see it as a title, but when you try to download it, you are informed that it is not yet supported on the iPad.

Reading Magazines on Your NOOK Color

In addition to books, B&N provides magazine subscriptions for your NOOK Color. B&N automatically delivers subscription content to your NOOK Color if a Wi-Fi connection is available. For more information on subscribing to content on your NOOK Color, **see** Chapter 9.

B&N recognizes that many magazines are more image intensive than ebooks, and the NOOK Color takes full advantage of that to display a rich reading environment for magazines. Often, magazines are read in landscape mode (see Figure 3.17), though portrait mode works as well.

FIGURE 3.17 Reading magazines is best in landscape view.

> NOTE: Some magazines function more like newspapers (for example, *The New York Review of Books*), so if you encounter a magazine like that, use the "Reading Newspapers on Your NOOK Color" section for more appropriate instructions.

> CAUTION: Some magazines (for example, *The New Yorker*) work only on the original NOOK. These will probably be updated in the near future to also work on the NOOK Color.

When you open a magazine, you can use pinch and zoom techniques to narrow in on pages. If you tap the page, you see the Thumbnail view at the bottom of the page (see Figure 3.18). This is a thumbnail of each page that you can scroll through. Tap the thumbnail to go to that page.

FIGURE 3.18   Scroll through a magazine's pages in Thumbnail view.

Pinching and zooming and dragging can be tedious for reading articles, and this is where the Article View comes in handy. When you see that button, tap Article View, and a secondary reading window opens on top of the magazine (see Figure 3.19). This is the text of the article (with an opening image) that you can scroll through to read more easily. Tap the X to close Article View. The good news is that your NOOK Color remembers where you were in the article, so if you tap Article View again for that article, it takes you to where you last stopped reading. You can also swipe left and right to navigate from article to article.

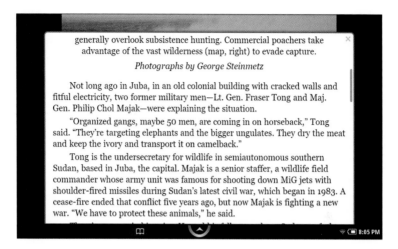

generally overlook subsistence hunting. Commercial poachers take advantage of the vast wilderness (map, right) to evade capture.

Photographs by George Steinmetz

Not long ago in Juba, in an old colonial building with cracked walls and fitful electricity, two former military men—Lt. Gen. Fraser Tong and Maj. Gen. Philip Chol Majak—were explaining the situation.

"Organized gangs, maybe 50 men, are coming in on horseback," Tong said. "They're targeting elephants and the bigger ungulates. They dry the meat and keep the ivory and transport it on camelback."

Tong is the undersecretary for wildlife in semiautonomous southern Sudan, based in Juba, the capital. Majak is a senior staffer, a wildlife field commander whose army unit was famous for shooting down MiG jets with shoulder-fired missiles during Sudan's latest civil war, which began in 1983. A cease-fire ended that conflict five years ago, but now Majak is fighting a new war. "We have to protect these animals," he said.

FIGURE 3.19   Reading an article.

While in Article View, if you tap the screen in the article, a Reading Tools bar appears (see Figure 3.20). This is slightly more limited than for ebooks, containing only Content, Text, and Brightness controls.

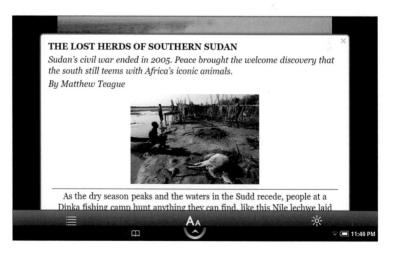

THE LOST HERDS OF SOUTHERN SUDAN

Sudan's civil war ended in 2005. Peace brought the welcome discovery that the south still teems with Africa's iconic animals.

By Matthew Teague

As the dry season peaks and the waters in the Sudd recede, people at a Dinka fishing camp hunt anything they can find, like this Nile lechwe laid

FIGURE 3.20   The Reading Tools bar in a magazine.

The Content option provides a table of contents for the magazine with brief descriptions of each article (see Figure 3.21). The Text and Brightness options are identical, excepting the Publisher Default option, as the Text and Brightness options for ebooks.

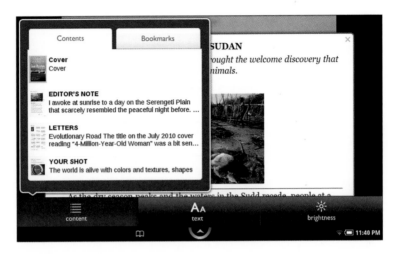

FIGURE 3.21   The contents of a magazine.

Reading Newspapers on Your NOOK Color

In addition to books, B&N provides newspaper subscriptions for your NOOK Color. B&N automatically delivers subscription content to your NOOK Color if a Wi-Fi connection is available.

For more information on subscribing to content on your NOOK Color, **see** Chapter 9.

Unlike books, newspaper content isn't presented in a linear format. Content is often presented as article headlines followed by a small synopsis of each article (see Figure 3.22). To read the specific article, tap the headline for that article. After an article is open, use swipe left and right gestures to navigate between pages just as you do when reading a book.

Tapping the screen displays the Reading Tools, which are the same as the ebook Read Tools (see Figure 3.23).

FIGURE 3.22   Reading a newspaper.

Tap to go to the front page of the newspaper.

Tap to go to the previous article.

Tap to go to the next article.

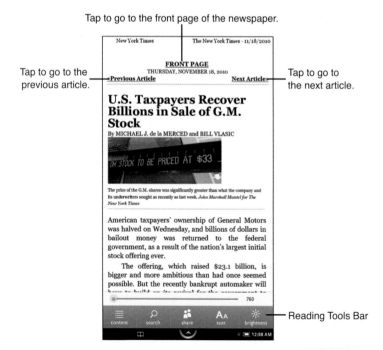

Reading Tools Bar

FIGURE 3.23   The Reading Tools bar is the same for ebooks and newspapers.

Many newspapers set their contents to go from section to section. Tap the Content button and tap the section (scroll if you need to) to go to that section (see Figure 3.24), where you can see a list of articles.

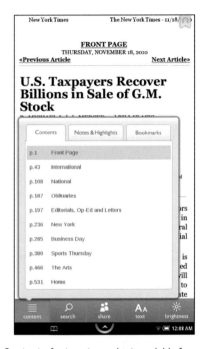

FIGURE 3.24 Use the Contents feature to navigate quickly from section to section.

Newspaper content often contains links that make navigating the content easier. For example, when reading *The New York Times*, you can move to the next or previous articles (as available) by tapping Previous Article or Next Article.

For more information on subscription content, including when your NOOK Color automatically deletes subscription content, **see** Chapter 9.

Reading NOOK Books for Kids on Your NOOK Color

One of the exciting things about the NOOK Color are the NOOK Books for Kids; many of them (and growing) feature Read to Me or Read and Play. If you shop for NOOK Books for kids, you see four formats for children's books:

- ▶ **NOOK Kids Read to Me**: The books have the enhanced Read to Me experience.

- ▶ **NOOK Kids (eBook)**: The regular NOOK Kids book lacks the Read to Me or Read and Play features, although it functions in every other way as a NOOK Book for Kids.

- ▶ **NOOK Kids Read and Play**: These books feature not only the Read to Me feature but also interactive activities. (For example, the narrator asks the child to tap the pig that is running, the child does so, and the running pig, well, runs.)

- ▶ **NOOK Kids Interactive**: These are Read and Play books, but with a different designation.

NOOK Books for Kids function differently than other content you read (or listen to) on the NOOK Color. The books open in landscape mode. The first page you are presented with has at least a Read by Myself button, though it can also have a Read to Me button (see Figure 3.25).

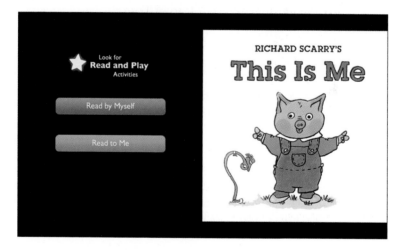

FIGURE 3.26 Tap Read to Me to have your NOOK Color read to you.

Read to Me opens the next page of the book, and you hear a voice reading the title (and not a mechanical voice). Each time you swipe to the next page, the voice reads the text on that page.

Read by Myself opens the next page of the book, but no voice begins reading. Instead, you can choose to have segments of the text read to you while you're reading if you want.

Picking either choice does not limit you to that choice again when you next open the book or return to the cover page. Also, Read and Play books do not have a specific choice to activate that option. When you open the book in either Read to Me or Read by Myself mode, the Read and Play activities are available.

NOOK Books for Kids features a Thumbnail view much like magazines (see Figure 3.26). Tap the upward pointing arrow to display the thumbnails. You can then scroll through these and tap the thumbnail you want to advance directly to that page. If you chose Read to Me, after that page opens, the reading begins. Tap the downward pointing arrow to hide the thumbnails.

FIGURE 3.26   NOOK Book for Kids' Thumbnail view.

If you tap a block of text, the text displays in a whitish balloon for easier reading. In addition, you see a right-pointing yellow arrow. Tapping that arrow reads to you that particular bit of text in that balloon. This works whether you chose Read to Me or Read by Myself earlier and does not alter what happens on the next page. In other words, if you chose Read by Myself, choosing to have a balloon of text read to you does not then activate Read to Me for the rest of the NOOK Book for Kids.

If you are reading a Read and Play NOOK Book, tap the Star button at the top of the page to begin the activities for that page. Just follow the instructions.

Tapping the Library button takes you back to the Home screen or Library (wherever you were last).

NOTE: NOOK Books for Kids are only available to read on the NOOK Color or the NOOK Kids for iPad™ app.

Reading Microsoft Office and Other Documents on Your NOOK Color

Beyond the NOOK Books, magazines, ebooks from other sources, and newspapers you can read, on your NOOK Color you can also read Microsoft Office documents, HTML files, and PDFs.

Reading Microsoft Office Documents

Your NOOK Color has Quickoffice installed, which is an application running on your NOOK Color that can open and read Microsoft Office documents.

> NOTE: You cannot *edit* the content of Office documents on your NOOK Color.

A great thing about this is you don't have to worry about which version of Word or Excel you have, you can open them up so long as they are valid Office documents. Have Word 2010 DOCX files? You can open these as easily as you open Word 2003 DOC files. No worries either between Mac or PC.

To open an Office document, tap Library from the Quick Nav Bar and tap My Files. You can then navigate to the location on either the NOOK Color or microSD card where your Office document is located. (Generally, these are in the My Files\Documents folder.)

You see a listing of files. You have two options at this point. Tapping the File icon opens the file. Pressing and holding the File icon displays a menu with Read, View Details, and Add to Shelf options, which are familiar options previously described in the chapter.

The different types of Office documents have some similar and some different options available when you open them, so now look at them individually.

Word

After the Word document opens, the Status bar adds two icons: Return and Reading Tools (see Figure 3.27). Tap the Return icon to undo the most recent action. (For example, if you tap it immediately after opening the document, you return to the folder from which you opened it.)

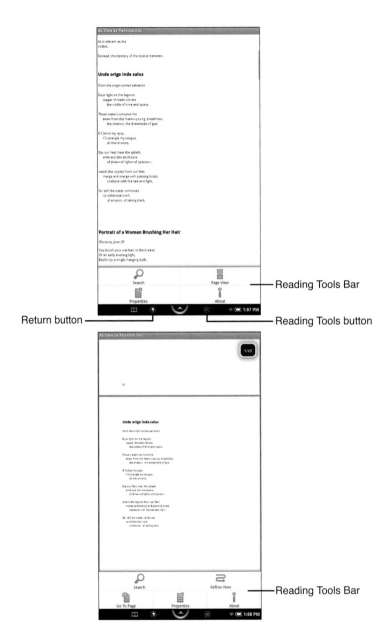

Reading Tools Bar

Return button —   — Reading Tools button

Reading Tools Bar

FIGURE 3.27   Reading Word documents on your NOOK Color.

Tap the Reading Tools icon to see a list of options:

- ▶ **Search**: Searches for words or phrases in the document.

- ▶ **Page View**: Displays individual pages versus continually flowing text. This option is available only when you are in Reflow view.

- ▶ **Reflow View**: Displays the text in continually flowing text. This option is available only when you are in Page view.

- ▶ **Go to Page**: Tap this and type the page number you want to go directly to. This option is available only when you are in Page view.

- ▶ **Properties**: Displays some basic information about the document.

- ▶ **About**: Shows information about Quickoffice.

While reading Word documents in either Page or Reflow view, you can use pinch and zoom to zoom in and out of the document. If you tap the reading screen, two zoom control buttons appear at the bottom of the page.

Excel

After the Excel document opens, the Status bar adds two icons: Return and Reading Tools. Tap the Return icon to undo the most recent action. (For example, if you tap it immediately after opening the document, you return to the folder from which you opened it.)

Tap the Reading Tools icon to see a list of options (see Figure 3.28):

- ▶ **Search**: Searches for words or phrases in the document.

- ▶ **Worksheet**: Opens a menu that enables you to move from worksheet to worksheet.

- ▶ **Go to Cell**: Opens a text entry screen. Type the cell (for example, D1) that you want to go to. The cell is then selected.

- ▶ **Properties**: Displays some basic information about the document.

- ▶ **About**: Shows information about Quickoffice.

While reading Excel documents, you can use pinch and zoom to zoom in and out of the document. If you tap the reading screen, two zoom control buttons appear at the bottom of the page.

The FX row at the top shows the formula or text in the selected cell. You cannot modify it, but you at least can see what is going into that cell.

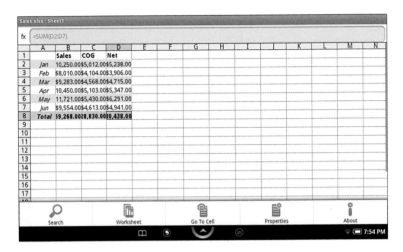

FIGURE 3.28   View Excel spreadsheets on your NOOK Color.

PowerPoint

After the PowerPoint document opens, the Status bar adds two icons: Return and Reading Tools. Tap the Return icon to undo the most recent action. (For example, if you tap it immediately after opening the document, you return to the folder from which you opened it.)

Tap the Reading Tools icon to see a list of options (see Figure 3.29):

▶ **Go to Slide**: Tap this and type the slide number you want to go directly to. This option is available only when you are in Page view.

▶ **Start Slideshow**: Start the slideshow. During the slideshow, which advances automatically through the slides, if you tap the screen, a slide control bar appears. Use this to pause or restart the slideshow or advance to the beginning or end slides or back and forth to the next slide. The Reading Tool icon also shows a Stop Slideshow button.

▶ **Properties**: Displays some basic information about the document.

▶ **About**: Shows information about Quickoffice.

While reading PowerPoint documents, you can use pinch and zoom to zoom in and out of the document. If you tap the reading screen, two zoom control buttons appear at the bottom of the page. Advancing through the slides is either done by either swiping (in portrait mode) or scrolling (in landscape mode).

FIGURE 3.29   Watch PowerPoint presentations on your NOOK Color.

Reading HTML Files

After you tap to open an HTML file, the HTML file is opened in the web browser. For more information about using the web browser, **see** Chapter 7, "Using NOOK Apps and Surfing the Web" for more information.

Reading PDFs

This section is specifically about PDFs outside of Adobe Digital Editions PDFs (ADE PDFs). ADE PDFs operate like regular ebooks.

Similar to Office documents, when a PDF opens, the Return and Reading Tools icons appear on the Status bar.

Tap the Reading Tools icon to see a list of options (see Figure 3.30):

▶ **Fit Page**: Tap this to have the page of the PDF fit within the entire screen. This works in either portrait or landscape mode.

▶ **Fit Width**: Shows the PDF page to fit the width of that page. (In general, this means that you get a closer view of the page, particularly in landscape mode.)

▶ **Go To Page**: Tap this and type the page number you want to go directly to.

▶ **Properties**: Displays some basic information about the document.

▶ **About**: Shows information about Quickoffice.

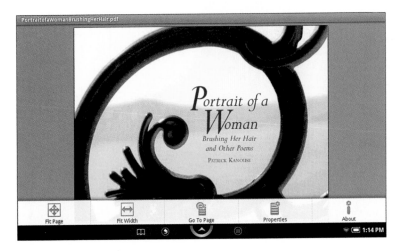

FIGURE 3.30   Reading a PDF document.

While reading PDF documents, you can use pinch and zoom to zoom in and out of the document. If you tap the reading screen, two zoom control buttons appear at the bottom of the page (see Figure 3.31).

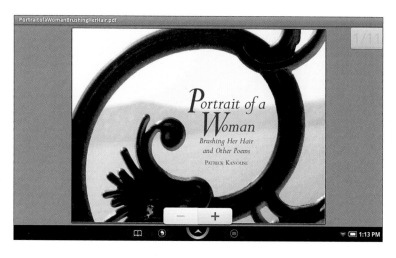

FIGURE 3.31   The Zoom controls for a PDF document.

CHAPTER 4

Lending and Borrowing Books with LendMe on Your NOOK Color

To keep readers from sharing ebooks with all their friends, publishers usually protect ebooks with digital rights management (DRM), which ties an ebook to an individual, and unless that individual can prove that he is an authorized reader, the ebook will not open.

DRM is one of the reasons some people don't like ebooks. After all, when readers find a good read, they like to pass it on to friends and family. The number of people with whom you can share a physical book is fairly limited, but because ebooks are digital copies of a book, they can be shared with millions of people quite easily via email, Facebook, and any number of other methods.

One of the unique features that B&N added to your NOOK Color is the ability to lend some NOOK Books to other readers using the LendMe feature. Although there are some restrictions when lending and borrowing books, the LendMe feature is a step in the right direction.

> TIP: If you receive a LendMe offer, the LendMe logo appears in the notification area of the NOOK Color. You can tap the logo, then tap the You Have a New LendMe Item link. From here, you can cancel the item (that is, make a decision later), decline the offer, or accept the offer.

Lending Books with LendMe

To lend a book to someone, the book must support LendMe. Not all books do. If a book does support lending, you see the LendMe logo on the book's page on bn.com, as shown in Figure 4.1. You also see the LendMe logo banner on the top-right corner of the cover on the NOOK Color and in the NOOK Apps.

⊞⊟ LendMe™   This NOOKbook is Lendable How it works

FIGURE 4.1   The LendMe logo appears on a book's page at bn.com if the book is lendable.

NOTE: When shopping for ebooks on your NOOK Color, the LendMe logo appears as a banner on the top-right cover of the cover, just like the covers on your NOOK Color.

The NOOK Color has many methods for lending books to your friends.

Lending from Your Library

If you are at the Home screen or in your library:

1. Press and hold the cover and then tap LendMe. The LendMe screen appears (see Figure 4.2).

FIGURE 4.2   Tap With Contacts or On Facebook to pick a friend to lend to.

2. Tap With Contacts or On Facebook. Either option gives you a similar screen (see Figure 4.3). The primary difference is the *method* the lend offer is communicated. If you choose With Contacts, the person is sent an email. If you choose On Facebook, the offer is posted on the person's wall (see Figure 4.4).

FIGURE 4.3   Select one of your Facebook friends.

FIGURE 4.4   The loan offer appears on your friend's wall.

3. Select a contact, or select Add Contact to add someone not currently in your contact list. Tap Next.

TIP: You can filter the Contacts list by tapping the Filter By option and choosing either All Contacts, Barnes & Noble, or Google. You can also type in the Search field to narrow the list by name.

TIP: Typed the name and selected the contact but you cannot move on to the next step? Tap the Hide Keyboard button. Now you can tap Next.

If you use the On Facebook option, tap Select Friend to see a list of your Facebook friends. Type in the Search field to narrow your search, select your friend, and tap Done.

4. Type a message to send with the lend invitation. (The message is optional.)

5. Tap Send or Post.

Your NOOK Color sends the offer and lets you know when it is successfully sent. The cover banner LendMe changes to Lent. Also, if you visit My NOOK Library, you can see details about when the offer was sent, who is borrowing it, and when it will be back to your library (see Figure 4.5).

FIGURE 4.5   The loan status on My NOOK Library.

NOTE: If you press and hold a cover and tap View Details, you have a LendMe option there as well. Tap LendMe and then follow the previous steps.

Lending from LendMe in the Library

If you tap Library from the Quick Nav Bar, you see LendMe as an option. Tap LendMe. The screen shows a series of shelves. Swipe left or right to move back and forth among the covers on the shelf. The three shelves are Borrowed, Books Available for Lending, and Lent to Others. You can also tap the large red banner at the top that takes you to the LendMe app (see the section "Lending Using the NOOK Friends App" for more information about the LendMe app). To lend books, follow the steps in the section "Lending from Your Library."

Rules for Lending

Choose carefully when lending a book because after you lend a NOOK Book, you can never lend that particular NOOK Book to anyone again. However, a NOOK Book is considered to be on loan only if your friend accepts the LendMe offer. If your friend rejects the offer or if she allows the offer to expire without accepting it, you can lend the NOOK Book again after it's returned to your library.

FIGURE 4.6 The LendMe screen.

I Want to Lend a NOOK Book to One of My Friends. Does My Friend Have to Own a NOOK Color for Me to Lend Her a NOOK Book?

No. Your friend can read a NOOK Book you've lent to her using the NOOK Apps, or original NOOK. However, your friend cannot read the book unless the email address you used to send the LendMe offer is associated with her B&N account.

The person to whom you've loaned the NOOK Book has 7 days to accept the loan offer. If she doesn't accept within 7 days, the book is returned to your library. The loan offer can also be rejected, in which case the book is returned to your library immediately.

A NOOK Book is loaned for 14 days, and while it is on loan, Lent appears on the cover and you cannot read the book. When you loan a book, you also loan your DRM rights to the book. Only one person can possess the DRM rights to a book at any one time, so you need to wait until the book is returned to your library before you can read the book again.

> CAUTION: There is no way to cancel a LendMe offer.

Borrowing Books

When a friend lends you a book, you receive a notification of the offer (see Figure 4.7). You have 7 days to either accept the offer or reject it. You can accept or reject the loan offer from your NOOK Color, original NOOK, or any of the NOOK Apps.

FIGURE 4.7 Versions of the same offer on different NOOK devices: NOOK for iPad™, NOOK for iPhone® , NOOK for PC™ app, My NOOK Library, and NOOK Color.

If you accept a loan offer from your NOOK Color, that book is also available for the loan period in NOOK Apps or original NOOK, and vice versa.

You can determine how much time is left on your loan period by looking at the cover. You see a number in the bottom right that indicates the number of days left. If you press and hold the cover and tap View Details, the price of the NOOK Book appears. You can tap the price to purchase the NOOK Book.

Lending Using the NOOK Friends App

You need to understand that the NOOK Friends app is related but separate from the LendMe program. This section covers the LendMe features of the NOOK Friends app; for the social features of the NOOK Friends app, see Chapter 8, "Using the Social Features of Your NOOK Color," for more information about this app.

If you have a circle of friends with NOOK Colors, you can see what NOOK Books they have available to lend and make a request. Here's how you do this:

1. From the Quick Nav Bar, tap Apps. Then tap NOOK Friends. Alternatively, from the Library, tap LendMe and then tap the Borrow Books from Friends with the NOOK Friends Beta button. The NOOK Friends app opens (see Figure 4.8).

FIGURE 4.8   The NOOK Friends app on the LendMe tab.

2. Tap either Lend, Borrow, Offers, or Requests depending on how you want to view what's available:

   ▶ **Lend**: Shows the NOOK Books you can lend.

   ▶ **Borrow**: Shows the NOOK Books your friends have available for borrowing.

   ▶ **Offers**: Shows NOOK Books friends have offered to lend you.

   ▶ **Requests**: Shows NOOK Books your friends have requested to borrow.

3. If you tap Lend, you see the available books you can lend. Tap LendMe to begin the process to lend a NOOK Book to a friend. Tap With Contacts or On Facebook to open a screen to select the person. Enter a message if you want and tap Send. The person sees a request like that shown in Figure 4.9.

4. If you tap Borrow, you see the available books you can borrow. Tap Borrow again, and tap Request to ask to borrow this NOOK Book. Enter a message if you want and tap Send. Type a message and tap Send. The request is sent. They see a request like that shown in Figure 4.10.

5. If you receive a lend offer, you can open the NOOK Friends app, tap LendMe, and tap Offers, where you see what NOOK Books are offered you. Tap View Offer. Here you can cancel the request (thus, postponing the decision until later), decline the offer, or accept it (see Figure 4.9).

FIGURE 4.9   Decline or accept a LendMe offer.

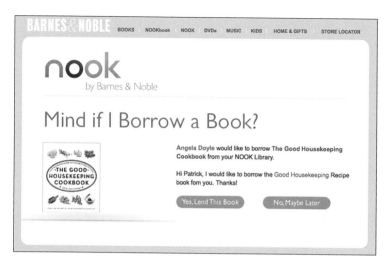

FIGURE 4.10 A friend is requesting to borrow a book.

If you tap the Settings button, you can choose to show certain NOOK Books to your friends (see Figure 4.11). If you want to hide a NOOK Book from lending, tap Show. The slider changes to Hide. You can change this back by tapping Hide.

FIGURE 4.11 Hide books from your friends so they cannot borrow it.

NOTE: You must be connected to a Wi-Fi hotspot to refresh the available books or alter the LendMe visibility. If you are not connected to a hotspot, tapping either button opens a Network Settings screen for you to choose a hotspot, if available.

Why would you want to hide a book from lending? You may be reading it at this moment and don't want to decline a request, or you may have a friend you know wants to borrow the book. Because the book can only be lent once, you want to remove it from view so that others cannot request it and you, again, have to decline.

CHAPTER 5

Using Highlights, Bookmarks, and Annotations

Take a look at one of your favorite books, and you can likely find notes in the margins and perhaps dog-eared pages. Jotting down notes about passages that impact you or marking pages you want to come back to visit later is how you make books a personalized possession. Fortunately, you don't have to forgo these things when it comes to ebooks, because your NOOK Color lets you easily highlight passages and add bookmarks and notes to pages.

> NOTE: Your NOOK Color, original NOOK, NOOK Apps, Barnes & Noble eReader for the Mac and Blackberry, and NOOK Study all support adding highlights and notes. However, notes and highlights entered in the eReader software or on the original NOOK are not shared with other devices. On the NOOK Color, NOOK Apps, and NOOK Study, if you add a note or highlight on one device, that note or highlight is available on another device—except for the original NOOK and Barnes & Noble eReader app.

Using Highlights, Notes, and Bookmarks on Your NOOK Color

When you think of highlighting something in a book, you typically think of using a yellow highlighter marker to draw attention to portions of the text. Highlighting on your NOOK Color is similar to that...but with a highlighter that has multiple colors all in one.

> TIP: Highlighting and notes are not supported for magazine content. You can add only highlights and notes in ebooks that support them. Caveat: Magazines that are more like newspapers (for example, *The New York Review of Books*) do support highlighting and notes.

A note in an ebook is simply a highlighted area with a message attached. Therefore, the steps necessary to add, view, edit, and delete notes are the same as the steps for using highlights.

Adding a Highlight or a Note

To highlight text or add a note in an ebook, follow these steps:

1. Press and hold a word. The word appears in a bubble, and that is your signal to raise your finger. The word is highlighted and the Text Selection toolbar appears.

2. If you want to highlight only that word, move to step 3. If you want to highlight a block of text, notice the highlighted word is bounded by two blue bars. Press, hold, and drag one of the blue bars to the location you want to end the highlight (see Figure 5.1).

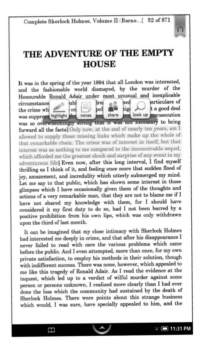

FIGURE 5.1   Highlight the text you want to add a note to.

NOTE: The initial word highlighted must always be the first or last word in the highlight.

3. Tap Highlight to just add a highlight. Tap Note if you want to add a note. If you chose the former, the text is highlighted. If you chose the latter, the Edit Note screen appears (see Figure 5.2).

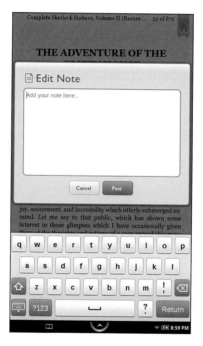

FIGURE 5.2 Enter your note.

4. Type your note and tap Post.

5. The highlight is added and a Note icon appears next in the margin (see Figure 5.3).

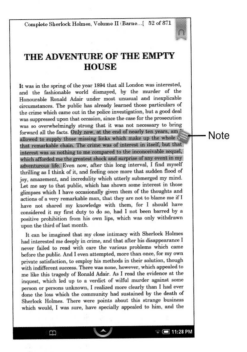

FIGURE 5.3   Your note is added.

Viewing, Editing, and Deleting Highlights and Notes

The simplest way to edit a note is to tap the highlighted text. A pop-up menu appears (see Figure 5.4), giving you several options:

▶ **View Note**: Tap this to view the note. This appears only if a note is attached to that highlight. After you are in the note, you can tap Edit to edit the note.

▶ **Edit Note**: Tap this to edit the text of the note. This appears only if a note is attached to that highlight.

▶ **Add Note**: Tap this to add a note to highlighted text. An Add Note screen appears. Type in your note and tap Post. This appears only if no note is attached to that highlight.

▶ **Remove Note**: Tap this to remove the note. The highlight will remain. This appears only if a note is attached to that highlight.

▶ **Remove Highlight**: Tap this to delete both the note and highlight.

▶ **Change Color**: Tap the color you want to change the color of the highlight for that particular one. You can use all three colors for highlights in the same ebook.

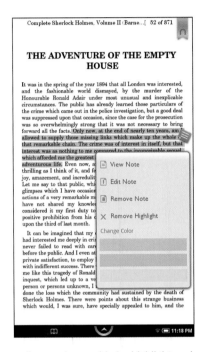

FIGURE 5.4   Your options after you have added a highlight and note.

> **TIP:** You can view the note text by tapping the Note icon on the page. From there, you can then tap Edit to edit the text of the note.

To navigate or jump to notes throughout an ebook, from the Reading Tools toolbar (tap the screen), tap Content. Then tap Notes & Highlights. You see a listing of the notes in the ebook (scroll if you need to see more), as shown in Figure 5.5. You see the text that was highlighted, the page number of the note, and the date and time it was last edited. Tap the particular note you want to jump to. The contents screen disappears, and you are taken to the page with the highlight or note you tapped.

A couple of other notes about this screen's contents. Two other options exist: Clear All and Notes & Highlights On/Off. If you tap Clear All, you delete all notes and highlights in the ebook. If you turn Notes & Highlights to Off, you turn off the visibility of the highlights, though the Note icon stays in the margin. You can turn Notes & Highlights back to On to have the highlights reappear.

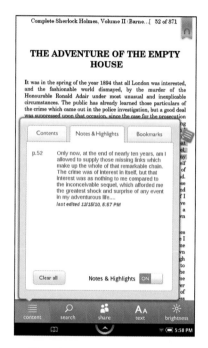

FIGURE 5.5   Jump to a specific note.

Using Bookmarks

Bookmarks enable you to easily return to a particular page. Unlike notes, bookmarks do not have any text associated with them. Bookmarks work in all your ebooks, magazines, and newspapers. Bookmarks are not supported in subscription content.

For ebooks and newspapers (and magazines that read like newspapers), to add a bookmark on the page you're reading, tap the reading screen, and then tap the icon that looks like a bookmark in the top right corner. It drops down a bit and changes to blue. Tap it again to remove the bookmark. Alternatively, you can tap the upper-right corner of the screen to place a bookmark or tap the bookmark to remove it.

For magazines, to add a bookmark on the page you're reading, you must be in portrait view. Tap the reading screen and then tap the + icon in the top-right corner (see Figure 5.6). It folds down. (Think of flipping the corner of a page in a book.) Tap it again to remove the bookmark. You cannot add bookmarks or remove individual bookmarks in landscape view.

Tap to add bookmark.

FIGURE 5.6   Bookmarks in magazines.

To return to a bookmark, from the Reading Tools toolbar, tap Content and then tap Bookmarks. A list of pages containing bookmarks appears (see Figure 5.7). Tap the bookmark you want to go to; your NOOK Color immediately takes you to that page.

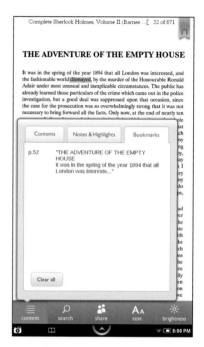

FIGURE 5.7   Jump to a specific bookmark.

To remove a bookmark, tap Clear All to remove all bookmarks in that ebook, magazine, or newspaper.

CHAPTER 6

Playing Music, Audiobooks, Podcasts, and Videos

For those of you who love to read, almost nothing stirs up as much nostalgia as the thought of listening to some nice music while reading a good book and maybe sipping a nice glass of wine. Your NOOK Color can't make wine, but it can provide the other two ingredients to this nostalgic scene.

NOTE: You can also listen to music via the online radio service, Pandora. To learn more about using Pandora, **see** Chapter 7's section "Playing Music with Pandora on Your NOOK Color."

Adding Audio Files to Your NOOK Color

The Music folder on your NOOK Color is used specifically for audio files (whether on the NOOK Color itself or on the microSD card). When you add audio files to this folder, your NOOK Color recognizes the files and enables you to play the audio using its built-in audio player.

NOTE: Your NOOK Color supports the following audio file types: MP3, AAC, MID, MIDI, M4A, WAV, and AMR. The best options are MP3 and AAC given their ubiquitous presence.

Playing Audio on Your NOOK Color

To play audio on your NOOK Color, you first need to copy the MP3 files to its memory or to a microSD card in your NOOK Color. Audio files should be copied into the Music folder (My Files\Music). If your microSD card does not have a Music folder, create one before copying audio files to it.

> **TIP:** If you haven't done so already, first load your music into a music player on your desktop or laptop (iTunes, Media Player, and so on). Doing so enables you to set album and artist name, and so on, which affects how easy it is to navigate your music in the Music Player on your NOOK Color.

After you copy your audio files to the Music folder, you can play them using the music player on your NOOK Color.

Using the Music Player

The Music Player on your NOOK Color is a basic music player. So if you're expecting an iPod on your NOOK Color, you'll be disappointed. However, for playing background music while reading and for listening to audiobooks and podcasts, your NOOK Color's Music Player is a great feature.

To launch the music player, from the Quick Nav Bar, tap Apps and then tap Music. The Music Player has two views for you to interact with your music: Browse and Now Playing (see Figure 6.1). If Browse appears in the top-right corner, you are in Now Playing view and vice versa.

FIGURE 6.1   Browse view in Music Player.

NOTE: Now Playing view is only available when a piece of music has been selected to play.

TIP: The speakers on your NOOK Color are mono and don't produce great sound. You'll hear better audio if you use headphones or ear buds plugged into the mini-jack at the top of your NOOK Color.

The following buttons are available just above the typical music control buttons in the Music Player in Browse view from left to right:

▶ **List**: Displays your music is alphabetical order (by name of the file). You can scroll through this list. Additionally, a small, fast Scroll icon appears on the right as you begin to scroll (see Figure 6.2). You can use this to scroll faster by pressing and dragging it up and down. You can use the Resort buttons on the left to drag a specific track up or down in the order. This last action permanently alters the order in this screen. Tap a track to begin playing.

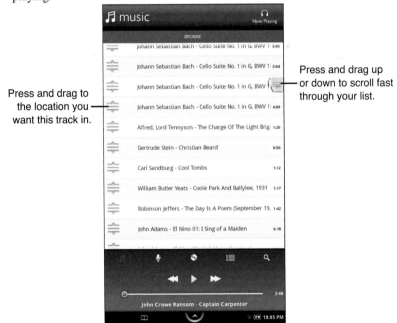

FIGURE 6.2 Viewing your music in a list.

▶ **Artist**: Displays your music according to artist. Tapping the artist name shows the albums associated with that artist. Tapping the album takes you to a List as in the previous bullet but only with that album. Tap a track to begin playing, and you go to the Now Playing view with the music playing.

▶ **CD**: Displays your music according to albums. Tapping the album takes you to a List as in the previous bullet but only with that album. Tap a track to begin playing, and you go to the Now Playing view with the music playing.

▶ **Browse**: Displays your music by most recently added.

▶ **Search**: Tapping this lets you search for artist, album, and so on. Tapping a track starts playing the track and takes you to Now Playing view. Tapping an album or artist takes you to the appropriate Album or Artist screen in Browse view.

You also have your typical music player controls:

▶ **Location in Track/Total Track Time**: Informational items only. The time listed on the left shows the time location within the track. The time on the right shows the total track time.

▶ **Play/Pause**: If the Music Player is playing audio, tapping this button pauses the audio. Otherwise, it resumes playing the audio.

▶ **Previous/Next Track**: Tapping this button takes you either to the previous or next track.

▶ **Scrubber**: The scrubber enables you to change the position in the current audio file quickly. Drag your finger on the scrubber to change the position. When you lift your finger from the touchscreen, the track plays from that location.

The following buttons (see Figure 6.3) above the typical music control buttons are available in the Music Player in Now Playing view:

TIP: If the button color is red, that feature is activated (that is, in use). If the button color is white, that particular feature is not active.

▶ **Shuffle**: Toggles shuffle mode on or off. Each time shuffle is toggled on, a new random order is created for the currently playing tracks.

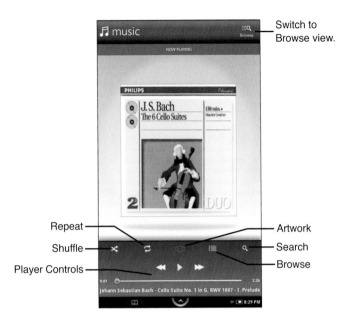

FIGURE 6.3   Now Playing view in Music Player.

▶ **Repeat**: Tapping once colors the button red, but the repeat is not activated. Tap again. A 1 appears in the center of the button. Repeat is now on. Note that it repeats the track endlessly…not just once.

▶ **Artwork**: The artwork for the track being played. (If none is available, a large music icon appears.)

▶ **Browse**: Displays your music by name. Additionally, a small, fast Scroll icon appears on the right as you begin to scroll. You can use this to scroll faster by pressing and dragging it up and down. You can use the Resort buttons on the left to drag a specific track up or down in the order. This last action permanently alters the order in this screen.

▶ **Search**: Tapping this lets you search for artist, album, and so on. Tapping a track starts playing the track and takes you to Now Playing view. Tapping an album or artist takes you to the appropriate Album or Artist screen in Browse view.

You also have your typical music player controls as indicated earlier.

While playing audio, you can tap the X button in the audio player to close the audio player interface. Your audio continues playing, but you can interact with other menus on your NOOK Color. To stop the audio from playing, tap the Pause button prior to closing the audio player.

TIP: Don't want to mess with opening up the Music Player, and such? From the Quick Nav Bar, tap Library, tap My Files, navigate to the Music folder, find the track you want to play, and tap that file. The Music Player opens and begins playing that track.

Playing Podcasts and Audiobooks on Your NOOK Color

In addition to listening to music, you can also use the audio player on your NOOK Color to play podcasts and audiobooks.

Podcasts

Podcasts are audio programs released on a regular schedule. You can subscribe to a podcast using any number of software applications, and when a new episode is released, it's automatically downloaded to your computer.

Podcasts are available that cover just about every topic of interest that you can think of. For example, podcasts can help you use your computer or help you take better pictures. Some podcasts deliver the news daily or weekly and some podcasts cover entertainment gossip. Other podcasts enable you to listen to your favorite radio shows on demand whenever you want.

If you own an iPhone, iPad, or iPod, you almost certainly already have iTunes on your computer. iTunes lets you easily subscribe to podcasts. You can search or browse for podcasts in the iTunes store. If you own a Microsoft Zune, you can subscribe to podcasts using the Zune Marketplace. If you don't already have an application that you can use to subscribe to podcasts, you can download Juice, a free podcast receiver that makes finding and subscribing to podcasts easy. Juice is available from http://juicereceiver.sourceforge.net.

When you subscribe to a podcast, each time you launch your podcast application (whether that's iTunes, Zune, Juice, or some other application), it checks for new episodes. If it finds a new episode, it downloads it automatically to your computer. You can then copy that episode to your NOOK Color. You need to check the documentation and options for the software you use to determine where it stores podcasts it downloads.

TIP: Be sure that you subscribe to podcasts in MP3 format. Some podcasts offer an MP3 version and versions in other formats. Only MP3 podcasts work on your NOOK Color.

Podcasts should be copied to the Music folder on your NOOK Color. The podcast will be available when you start the Music Player on your NOOK Color.

Audiobooks

Audiobooks are recordings of someone reading a book out loud. They are the digital version of books on tape. The most popular source of audiobooks is Audible.com, but your NOOK Color is not compatible with Audible audiobooks. However, you can enjoy plenty of sources of MP3 audiobooks on your NOOK Color.

Following are sources of MP3 audiobooks you can use on your NOOK Color:

▶ **Audiobooks.org**: Free audiobook versions of some classic books. There aren't many books here, but the ones they offer are of good quality.

▶ **Simply Audiobooks (www.simplyaudiobooks.com/downloads)**: For a few dollars per month, you can download as many audiobooks as you want. Simply Audiobooks offers both MP3 and WMA audiobooks, so be sure you choose the MP3 versions for your NOOK Color.

▶ **B&N Audiobooks (www.barnesandnoble.com/subjects/audio)**: B&N offers a wide assortment of audiobooks. If you're a B&N member, you can get some great deals for your NOOK Color.

▶ **Google Product Search**: Google Product Search (www.google.com/prdhp) is an excellent way to locate MP3 audiobooks. Simply search for "mp3 audiobook," and you can find a vast assortment from many merchants.

After you download an audiobook, copy it to the Music folder on your NOOK Color. You can then play it by selecting the file from the Media Player playlist.

> TIP: You can listen to most MP3 tracks in your music player. Check out the Teaching Company's (www.teach12.com) courses, many of which are available as audio downloads. As noted, always choose the MP3 version of files.

Playing Video Files on Your NOOK Color

No similar video player exists for videos as for music; however, watching videos on your NOOK Color is easy. The ideal video format is MP4, though 3gp, 3g2, m4v, and OGG also work. You may want to have QuickTime Pro or another bit of software available to convert video to the MP4 format (assuming it is not DRM protected).

NOTE: Although the B&N website says that only MP4 is supported, the user manual included on the NOOK Color indicates that the other formats are supported. The user manual is *more* correct because the NOOK Color does support those formats.

I have had trouble getting some video to play—a blank screen with a Back button shows and that's it. I had the most success, by far, taking my Flip camera videos and converting them among the various formats and getting them to play with sound. (Though, I had more trouble with the OGG format than any.) DRM protected videos are even more troublesome. If you have a video that you can copy, rip it to your computer using MP4. That's your best bet. I expect improved video support capabilities will be available with future firmware updates.

To play a video on your NOOK Color, you first need to copy the files to its memory or to a microSD card in your NOOK Color. The files should be copied into the Videos folder (My Files\Videos). If your microSD card does not have a Videos folder, create one before copying audio files to it.

To play a video on your NOOK Color, from the Quick Nav Bar, tap Library and then the My Files tab. Open the My Files folder in the list, navigate to the Videos folder, find the video you want to play, and tap the video (see Figure 6.4). The video opens with controls familiar to videos and a Back button. (Tapping this takes you back to the Videos folder.)

TIP: Have a TiVo? I do (actually, more than one). You can transfer the TV shows from TiVo to your laptop and then place these (in MP4 format) onto your NOOK Color—TV wherever you go!

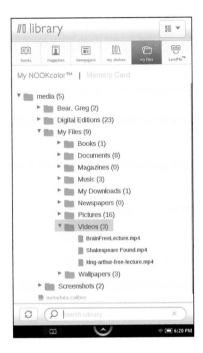

FIGURE 6.4 Navigate to the Videos folder and tap a video to play it.

CHAPTER 7

Using NOOK Apps and Surfing the Web

The NOOK Color includes a markedly improved web browser experience over the original NOOK's browser. Also, B&N added NOOK Apps (called NOOKextras until the April 2011 firmware 1.2.0 release), which include games, the Music Player you learned about in Chapter 6, "Playing Music, Audiobooks, Podcasts, and Videos," and other items.

Using NOOK Apps

If you have an iPhone, iPad, or Android phone, you are familiar with these download-able programs you can add to those devices. Well, a NOOK App is an app created specifically for the NOOK Color.

> NOTE: Though it is an Android-based device, you cannot download and use apps from the Android marketplace. That is...unless you root your NOOK Color. Rooting means a legal form of hacking, and rooting your NOOK Color is easy. **See** Chapter 10, "Rooting Your NOOK Color," for how.

You can get NOOK Apps by tapping Apps from the Quick Nav Bar. B&N preloaded several NOOK Apps to your NOOK Color (see Figure 7.1):

- ▶ **Chess**: Tap this to play some chess.
- ▶ **Contacts**: Tap this to see the list of your contacts, both B&N and Google (if you linked your Google contacts).
- ▶ **Crossword**: Tap this to play a crossword puzzle from *The New York Sun*.
- ▶ **Email**: A full-featured email application.
- ▶ **Gallery**: Tap this to open up an app to view images on the NOOK Color.

▶ **NOOK Friends**: Tap this to open this social networking app, which includes LendMe options. **See** Chapter 8, "Using the Social Features of Your NOOK Color," for more information about this app.

▶ **Music**: Tap this to open the Music Player (**see** Chapter 6 for more details about using the Music Player).

▶ **Pandora**: Tap this to open the Pandora application and listen to music.

▶ **Sudoku**: Tap this to play a game of Soduko.

FIGURE 7.1   The NOOK Apps on your NOOK Color.

Tap Discover More NOOK Apps to open the B&N store on the apps page. (For more information about shopping for apps, **see** Chapter 9, "Shopping and Visiting B&N on Your NOOK Color.")

If you tap the Sync button, your NOOK Color connects with B&N and determines if any updates are available for your existing apps. The Available Updates screen appears. You can choose to update all, some, or none of your apps.

For apps you have added beyond the standard, if you press and hold the app, you see some options similar to ebooks (see Figure 7.2).

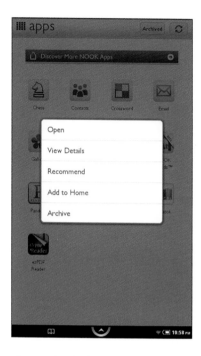

FIGURE 7.2 The Options for nonstandard apps.

The options are essentially the same as for ebooks with one difference. If you tap Archive, the app disappears from this screen. If you tap the Archived button, the Archived Apps screen appears and shows you all your archived apps. Press and hold the app icon, and then tap Unarchive to put it back on the NOOK Apps screen.

Playing Chess on Your NOOK Color

Feel like playing a game of chess? Well, your opponent is just a tap away. When you tap Chess in NOOK Apps, the game opens with the board displayed (see Figure 7.3). Tap Settings to set your color (Brown, Black, or Random). Brown moves first. In settings, you can also set the difficulty (Easy, Normal, or Hard). Finally, you can also set the amount of time allowed to win. On this latter setting, you can set it so that only you or the NOOK Color or both have a designated amount of time to win the game.

> NOTE: The time allowed is used up only when it is that player's turn. In other words, if you give yourself 5 minutes to win the game, your clock counts down only when it's your turn to move.

FIGURE 7.3   Take on the NOOK Color in a game of chess.

The game is straightforward to use. After starting the game, press and hold the piece you want to move, and drag to the spot you want it. The game does not let you make an illegal move. (It say "Wrong move!") If you mess up, you can tap Undo to go back to the previous positions.

If you tap Pause Game, you pause the game and can resume simply by tapping Resume Game. Also, if you leave the game to go read an ebook or magazine, you can return to the game by going to the Quick Nav Bar, tapping Apps, and tapping Chess.

Tap Resign to, well, you know…admit defeat.

Using Contacts on Your NOOK Color

If you linked your Google Contacts during the set up phase discussed in the Chapter 2 "Social Menu" section, you see them here (if you haven't already attempted to share quotes yet). Tap Contacts to open the Contacts app.

Here, you can filter your contacts by All, Barnes & Noble, and Google (see Figure 7.4). By default, all are shown. The Barnes & Noble set are contacts stored only on your NOOK Color. Google contacts are all your Google contacts (assuming you chose to link your Google account to your NOOK Color and use Google Contacts).

FIGURE 7.4   Filter your contacts to narrow your list.

TIP: Until I bought my NOOK Color, I did not use Google Contacts. But then I realized I didn't want to add a hundred contacts manually, so I went to where I kept my contacts (in this case, Mac's Address Book) and exported the contacts. I then imported them into Google Contacts (under Google Contacts' More Actions menu). I did it one time to get that.

NOTE: If you linked Google to your NOOK Color, you cannot edit the Google Contacts' information on the NOOK Color.

Use the Search Contacts box to search for a specific person, or you can scroll through your list.

If you want to add a B&N contact, tap Add Contact (see Figure 7.5). Fill in the First and Last Names, and add an email address. You can add more email addresses for that contact by tapping Add New Email. Tap Done when you have entered in all the information.

FIGURE 7.5   Adding a contact is easy.

If you need to later edit that contact, find it in your Contacts, tap the name, and then tap Edit. Adjust as necessary and tap Done.

Playing Crossword on Your NOOK Color

The NOOK Color features a crossword puzzle game featuring crosswords from *The New York Sun*. To play, from the Quick Nav Bar, tap Apps and then tap Crossword (see Figure 7.6). Tap Game and tap your difficulty level. A new puzzle appears. You can interact in several ways with the puzzle and enter your answers (or delete your mistakes).

You can tap any of the white cells in the puzzle. It highlights the word. The darker green cell is where any letter you type appears. Tap the cell again, and it switches to either the across or the down word.

The clues to the puzzles are at the top of the screen. If you tap that area, it expands and you can scroll through either the Across or Down list. Tap the clue to highlight the word in the crossword puzzle.

You can also navigate from word to word by tapping either the Prev Word or Next Word buttons at the bottom of the screen. This particular option cycles through the words depending on your current selection.

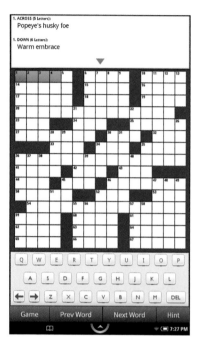

FIGURE 7.6 Play a crossword game to pass the time.

Tapping the particular word in the crossword is the easiest to move from word to word.

To enter your answer, tap the letters as appropriate. Tapping one letter enters that letter in the cell and then moves to the next cell for you to enter the letter. Tap DEL to delete the letter. Use the arrow keys to move from letter to letter in the word.

If you get stuck, you can tap Hint, and it enters the letter for the currently selected cell.

NOTE: At this time, there seems to be no way to check your puzzle's answers.

Using Email on Your NOOK Color

Email is a full-featured email app. Start Email by tapping Apps from the Quick Nav Bar. Then tap Email. The Email app appears. If this is the first time you are starting Email, you see the Welcome screen (see Figure 7.7).

Type in your email username and password. Your NOOK Color connects with the email provider. After a few seconds, you receive the Congratulations screen (see Figure 7.8).

FIGURE 7.7   The Email app Welcome screen.

FIGURE 7.8   The Email app Congratulations screen.

Update the Account Description if you want. Also, adjust the Email Account Name, which makes it easy to find whose email account it is if you share your NOOK Color. Tap Done.

The NOOK Color downloads your email in the Email app interface (see Figure 7.9).

FIGURE 7.9 The Email app interface.

Now become oriented to this interface (which is the screen you see initially, if you have already set up an account and then start the Email app):

- ▶ **Compose**: Tap this to compose an email.

- ▶ **Account**: Tap this to change which email account you want to view.

- ▶ **Folders**: Tap this to see a different folder (Inbox, Sent, ToKeep, and so on).

- ▶ **Email Check box**: Tap this to select an email to delete.

- ▶ **Delete**: Tap this to delete any selected emails.

- ▶ **Email**: Tap this to open the email.

▶ **Synch**: Tap this to connect with the email server to see if you have any new emails.

▶ **Search**: Tap this to search your email.

Now look at a few of these items in more detail.

Compose

Tapping the Compose button opens up the Compose Email screen (see Figure 7.10).

FIGURE 7.10   The Compose Email screen.

In the To box, either type the email address you want to send the email to or tap the Contacts button and select a contact (or contacts). If you want to CC or BCC an email address, tap the CC:/BCC: line. This expands into two separate text boxes: one for CC and one for BCC.

If you want a subject line for your email, tap the Subject text box, and type in the subject.

To begin typing your message, tap the large text box that states, Enter Message Here. Type the email. When you are ready to send, tap Send. If you want to cancel your email, simply tap Cancel. Currently a draft option is not available. (You can always just email yourself if you need to save an email in progress.)

Account

Tapping the Account button displays your existing accounts. Tap the account you want to shift to. Tap Accounts to add and modify accounts (see Figure 7.11).

FIGURE 7.11   The Accounts screen.

If you want to delete an account, tap the check box next to that account, and then tap the Delete button.

To add another account, tap Add Account. Enter your account information. If you want to make the new account the default account, tap the check box for Set as Default Account. Tap Next (the Next underneath the Set as Default Account option). Tap Done.

If you have more than one account and want to see all emails for all accounts in one screen, tap Accounts and then tap Combined Inbox.

Tap the Gear button to access settings for the email account (see Figure 7.12).

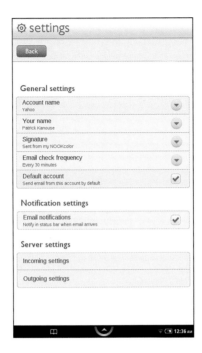

FIGURE 7.12   Email settings screen.

You have a variety of options to choose from here.

Email

After you tap an email, the email opens (see Figure 7.13).

You have a number of options here, but the options are typical of most email applications. Tap the Reply button; then tap Reply, Reply All, or Forward.

Tap Move To and then select a folder.

If an attachment is included, tap Open to save the attachment. First, the attachment is saved to your My Files\My Downloads folder. Second, the attachment opens in the appropriate software (Gallery for images, Reader for PDFs, QuickOffice for Word, and so on).

FIGURE 7.13   A typical email.

Using the Gallery on Your NOOK Color

Gallery is a photo gallery on your NOOK Color that displays JPG, GIF, PNG, or
BMP images.

NOTE: The Gallery app in its current incarnation is not very useful for this
reason: Gallery collects every JPG, GIF, PNG, or BMP on your NOOK Color and
microSD card and displays them here—every single one. If you have numerous
images for covers not from NOOK Books, when you open Gallery, you can see
all of them.

Start Gallery by tapping Apps from the Quick Nav Bar. Then tap Gallery. Your photos appear (see Figure 7.14). You can choose to look at them in either Picture or Grid
view. If you are in Picture view, in the top-right corner, you see an option called Grid
and vice versa. Tap this to switch to the other view. You can do most of your interac-
tion with images in Picture view. Grid view is useful for quickly navigating your
photos.

FIGURE 7.14 The gallery of images on your NOOK Color.

When you find a photo you want to see in Picture view, tap it. The image appears all alone on the screen then. You can still move between images in Picture view by swiping right or left. You can also use pinch and zoom techniques to zoom in and out.

Tap the image to display the Photo Tools bar (see Figure 7.15). You have six options here:

- ▶ **Slideshow**: Tap this option to start a slideshow. The screen shows only the image, and after a pause the next image appears. To see the order of the images, take a look at them in Grid view before starting the slideshow.

  To exit the slideshow, tap the Home button.

- ▶ **Wallpaper**: Tap this option to set this images as your Home screen image.

  After you tap Wallpaper, a version of the photo appears with an orange outlined box and two buttons: Save and Discard. The orange outlined box is for cropping the image to the size of the wallpaper. Whatever is *inside* the orange outlined box will be used for the wallpaper. To move that box, press and hold, and then drag it around to wherever you want it. Tap Save to make it the wallpaper, and return to Gallery, or tap Discard to exit back to Gallery.

FIGURE 7.15 Use the Photo Tools bar to manipulate your images.

▶ **Crop**: Tap this option crop the image to remove portions of it that you do not want. When you tap Crop, the photo appears with an orange outlined box and two buttons: Save and Discard (see Figure 7.16). Like making wallpaper, whatever is on the inside of the orange box is retained. With crop, however, you can tap the orange outline and drag it smaller or larger. Tap Save to make it the wallpaper and return to Gallery, or tap Discard to exit back to Gallery.

▶ **Left/Right**: These two buttons rotate the image either clockwise or counterclockwise. Use this if an image appears on its side and you want it right-side up.

▶ **Delete**: Tap this to delete the image from your NOOK Color.

FIGURE 7.16   Adjust the orange box to crop out what you don't want in the image.

Playing Music with Pandora on Your NOOK Color

On the original NOOK, one of the earliest hacks to it was to add a Pandora music player. Pandora is a web-delivered streaming music service, for free (Pandora.com). You create stations based on artists or types of music, and Pandora plays music from that artist or type of music and similar types of music—think of stations as playlists. You can create multiple stations. As you're listening to music, you can give it a thumbs up or down to indicate how well the selection matches your expectations to that station. Pandora uses this to refine the music it picks.

If you listen to Pandora on your NOOK Color, you can leave the app to read, surf the Internet, or do other things while Pandora continues to play.

> NOTE: You must be connected to a Wi-Fi hotspot and the Internet to listen to Pandora.

A couple of things to note about Pandora: Because it is free and the licenses it has signed with music distribution companies, you can skip a song that you don't like (by tapping the Next Song button or tapping thumbs down *while* the song is playing).

However, you are limited to 6 skips per station per hour and a total of 12 skips per day across all stations.

The first time you start Pandora on your NOOK Color, you can either enter existing account information and tap Login or register for a new account by tapping Register for Free (see Figure 7.17). If the latter, fill out the Create New Account information, and tap Register for Free.

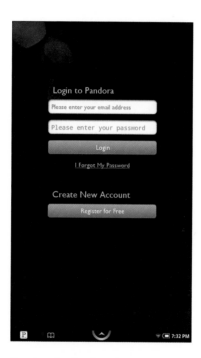

FIGURE 7.17   Setting up Pandora for the first time.

If you have an existing account, when you log in, the NOOK Color Pandora app grabs all your stations.

After the Pandora app starts, to add a station follow these steps:

1. Tap Add Station. The Add Station screen appears.

2. In the Artist, Song, or Composer field, type in what you are looking for. Tap Done.

3. Depending on your search, you may see many results or just a few. Tap the one that best meets your needs. Pandora switches to play mode and adds the station so that you can access it any time by tapping My Stations.

Tap My Stations to see a list of your stations (see Figure 7.18). Tap the station you want to listen to. Tap Edit and then the hyphen in a Circle icon at the left to delete that station.

FIGURE 7.18   Your Pandora stations.

While listening to music, you can use the thumbs up or down icons, bookmark a song or artist, pause playing, or tap skip to next song (see Figure 7.19).

> NOTE: If you are not viewing the Pandora application (that is, you're reading a book while Pandora is playing songs), you can always tap the Pandora Notification icon to see what is playing. If you tap the Notification icon, the Pandora app opens.

Playing Sudoku on Your NOOK Color

Sudoku is a wildly popular puzzle game, and the original NOOK had a Sudoku game (with release 1.3). You can continue to enjoy the pleasures of Sudoku on your NOOK Color. To play Sudoku, from the Quick Nav Bar, tap Apps, and then tap Sudoku.

FIGURE 7.19 The Pandora music player.

When you first start Sudoku, tap New Game (see Figure 7.20). Then tap which game difficulty you want. (If you have previously started a game and left it, you can either resume the existing game or tap New Game to start a new game.)

> NOTE: The difficulty of Sudoku is measured by the number of prefilled numbers you are provided.

A puzzle appears and you can begin play. You have two primary options for entering numbers: Pen and Notes. Notes enables you enter the possible numbers you think might fill that cell without committing to that number (see Figure 7.21). Pen enters that number as your choice. (You can easily overwrite it by choosing another or tapping Undo or Clear Cell.)

> TIP: If the number appears in red in the cell, that number is already used in that row and cannot be used again.

FIGURE 7.20   Play Sudoku to keep your mind sharp.

FIGURE 7.21   Use notes to help solve the puzzle as if you were writing it on paper.

Use the number pad to enter the numbers in either Pen or Notes mode. Undo cancels out your last action and redo reverts that back. For example, if you enter 3 in a cell and then enter 4, tapping Undo takes that cell back to 3. Tapping Redo returns it to 4. Tap Clear Cell to remove any numbers from the cell.

Tap Pause Game to stop the timer. You can then resume playing by tapping Resume Game or the arrow button in the center of the puzzle screen.

Tapping Quit Game quits that particular game, so you can play a new one.

If you leave the game to go read or surf the Internet, the game automatically pauses.

Browsing the Web with Your NOOK Color

The NOOK Color comes with a full-featured web browser (see Figure 7.22). With the 1.2.0 firmware release, the browser now supports Flash content. Flash content often appears on web pages in the form of videos or interactive animations and images (not all such images you see on web pages are Flash, but many are). One concern with Flash content is that it is power hungry and will use more battery power than standard web pages. Nonetheless, much content on the web is in Flash, though the number is decreasing.

FIGURE 7.22 The NOOK Color's web browser.

To start the browser, from the Quick Nav Bar, tap Web.

If you are familiar with the web browser on the original NOOK, forget what you knew. The NOOK Color browser is by far a better browser experience. The original NOOK's browser displayed the page on the E Ink and you navigated with the small touchscreen. This was tedious at best. The browser on the NOOK Color displays the whole page in color, allows you to tap links to navigate, and lets you pinch and zoom to specific locations on the web page.

> NOTE: To access web pages, you must be connected to a Wi-Fi hotspot.

An Overview of Browsing on Your NOOK Color

Browsing the web on your NOOK Color is easy. From the Quick Nav Bar, tap Web to open the browser. The browser opens to the home page or last page you were on.

At the top, you see a typical looking web browser interface:

- ▶ **Back Button**: Tap to go back to the previous web page.

- ▶ **Address Bar**: Tap to enter a new web address or search the web. Tapping gives you the keyboard, and you can either enter a specific web address, or you can type a search term. As you type, a series of tappable links appears below the bar. This displays previously searched terms and websites. You can continue typing and tap Go, which performs a Google search.

- ▶ **Stop Button**: Tap to stop the current page loading.

- ▶ **Bookmarks**: Tap to access bookmarks, most visited sites, and your history. For more information about the Bookmarks options, **see** "Using the Bookmarks Screen."

- ▶ **Options**: Tap to access additional options, settings, and so on. For more information about the Options, **see** "Using the Browser Options."

> NOTE: You can view web pages in either portrait or landscape mode.

When you are at a web page, press and hold, and then drag to maneuver the page. You can zoom into an area of the page by using the pinch and zoom gesture, tapping twice quickly on that area of the screen or tapping once and then using the plus button at the bottom of the screen.

To zoom back out, unpinch, tap twice on an area of the screen, or tap once and then use the minus button at the bottom of the screen.

> NOTE: To do a lot of the functions in the web browser, you have to wait for the page to load completely.

Tap a link to go to that link if it is a regular hyperlink (for example, going to another web page). Some links download items to your NOOK Color. For example, if you press and hold on an image, you can get a menu to save or view the image (see Figure 7.23). However, if you are at Project Gutenberg go to the download section for a specific book and tap the EPUB link, the file downloads to your NOOK Color (see Figure 7.24). These downloads go to the My Files\My Downloads folder.

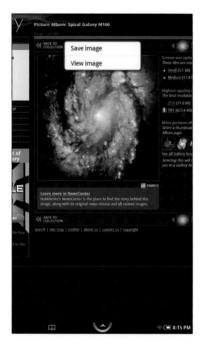

FIGURE 7.23   Some links offer you an opportunity to save or view the file.

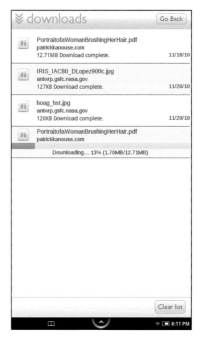

FIGURE 7.24   Some links download the file to your NOOK Color.

If you press and hold a hyperlink (see Figure 7.25), a menu appears with these options:

▶ **Open**: Opens the link. This is the same as tapping the link.

▶ **Open in New Window**: Opens the link in a new window, thus leaving your existing window in place.

▶ **Bookmark Link**: Adds a bookmark to the link you are pressing.

▶ **Copy Link URL**: Copies the link to the Clipboard.

> NOTE: In the browser, copying text or links is allowed in a couple of places. However, I have yet to find a place where I can paste the said text.

FIGURE 7.25 Your options after you press and hold a hyperlink.

If you press and hold in a nonlink area of the web page, a menu appears with these options (see Figure 7.26):

▶ **Find on Page**: Tap this to search for specific text on this page. The keyboard appears. Type in what you want to search for. Tap Search. The keyboard drops away and the number of occurrences found on the page is shown. If more than one appearance is on the page, use the back and forward buttons to highlight the word.

▶ **Select Text**: Tap this to select text on the page. After you tap Select Text, press at the starting point of the text you want to select, and drag to the ending of the text. Lift your finger, and you receive a note that the text has been copied to the Clipboard.

NOTE: Because it is a web page, sometimes when selecting text, you grab a couple of columns, and so on. It's imperfect and, given that I have yet to find the place to paste the text, I'm not sure of the point as yet.

FIGURE 7.26   Your options after you press and hold a nonhyperlink area on a web page.

▶ **Page Info**: Tap this to see some information related to the page.

▶ **Settings**: Tap this to access the browser settings. For more information about the Options, **see** "Using the Browser Options."

▶ **Downloads**: Tap this to see any downloads you have made from the NOOK Color to the My Downloads folder.

▶ **Bookmark This Page**: Tap this to add this page to your bookmarks.

Using the Bookmarks Screen

The Bookmarks screen, shown in Figure 7.27, enables you to add bookmarks, modify existing ones, and other options. The screen opens with three tabs: Bookmarks, Most Visited, and History.

To get to the Bookmarks screen, tap the Bookmarks button. The Bookmarks screen opens at the Bookmarks tab. The bookmarks are thumbnails of the web pages. The top-left thumbnail, with Add overlaid on it, is actually not yet a bookmark. You can make this a bookmark by tapping it. The Add Bookmark window appears. You can adjust the name of the bookmark and location. (I recommend leaving this as is.) Tap OK to make it a bookmark.

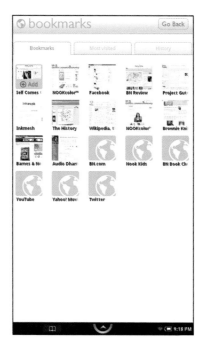

FIGURE 7.27   The Bookmarks screen.

The other thumbnails are your bookmarks. Tap the thumbnail to open that web page. If you press and hold the thumbnail, a pop-up menu provides these options (see Figure 7.28):

- ▶ **Open**: Opens the link. This is the same at tapping the link.

- ▶ **Open in New Window**: Opens the link in a new window, thus leaving your existing window in place.

- ▶ **Edit Bookmark**: Opens the Edit Bookmark window. Here you can adjust the name and location (that is, the hyperlink address) of the bookmark.

- ▶ **Copy Link URL**: Copies the link to the clipboard.

- ▶ **Delete Bookmark**: Deletes the bookmark. You will be asked to confirm that you want to delete it.

- ▶ **Set as Homepage**: Sets this bookmark as your home page.

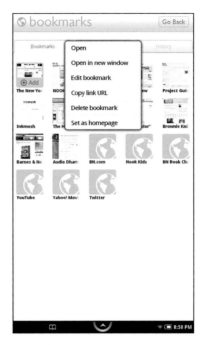

FIGURE 7.28   Additional options on the Bookmarks screen.

The Most Visited tab lists the web pages you have visited the, well, most often. A star appears to the right of the link. Gold means that it is a bookmark. Gray means that it is not a bookmark.

You can tap a link to go to that web page. If you press and hold the link, you see a set of options similar to the preceding list of options with one exception: Delete Bookmark is replaced by Remove from History. Tapping this removes the web page from your history.

> NOTE: You might think that tapping Remove from History would remove the link from the History tab on the Bookmarks screen. Although logical, you would be incorrect to think this. On the Most Visited tab, the Remove from History option is better labeled Remove from Most Visited.

The History tab lists the web pages you have visited. A star appears to the right of the link. Gold means that it is a bookmark. Gray means that it is not a bookmark. Scrolling down to the bottom of the list provides options for sites visited Yesterday, 5 Days Ago, and 1 Month Ago. Tapping one of those reveals more sites.

You can tap a link to go to that web page. If you press and hold the link, you see a set of options similar to the previous list of options. Tapping Remove from History removes the web page from the history.

On the screen, you can also tap Clear History to wipe out the entire history at once.

Using the Browser Options

As mentioned previously, tap the Options button to access browser settings and other options (see Figure 7.29). The following appears in the drop-down menu:

- ▶ **New Window**: Tap this to open a new window and leave the current window in place.

- ▶ **Bookmarks**: Tap this to open the Bookmarks screen. For more information about the Bookmarks options, **see** "Using the Bookmarks Screen."

- ▶ **Windows**: Tap this to see all the windows currently open. Tap the window you want to go to. Tap the X button to close that window.

- ▶ **Refresh**: Tap this to refresh the page, which is particularly useful if the page receives periodic updates.

- ▶ **Forward**: If you have tapped the Back button, tap Forward to go back to the previous page.

- ▶ **More Options**: Provides many items already covered, except for Settings.

Many settings about the web browser are available. Most of them are self-explanatory, but a few are covered in detail here.

Tap Text Size to adjust how large the text appears on web pages. Consider this the same as adjusting the text size in ebooks. You have several options: Tiny, Small, Normal, Large, and Huge.

Tap Default Zoom to set how the browser opens pages initially. You have three options: Far, Medium, and Close. Far shows more of the web page than the other two, which means that you have to zoom in more to get close. Close starts in very close, usually requiring more pressing and dragging to maneuver around the page.

> TIP: I think Medium is the best setting. If you use Far, when you double-tap quickly a part of the page, the page zooms in quickly equivalent to the Close setting size. Medium seems to strike the right balance between easy visibility without being too close.

FIGURE 7.29   The browser's Options screen.

The Open Pages in Overview setting determines how newly opened pages first appear. If this setting is turned on, the web page appears in the browser showing the page in a zoomed out view (though not equivalent to the Far setting in Default Zoom).

With the Open in Background setting off, when you choose to open a link in a new window, that new window is what you see. With this setting on, that new window is hidden until you choose it by tapping Options and then tapping Windows.

You can use the Set Homepage option here to set the current web page as the home page.

The NOOK Color's web browser is, as you have learned, feature rich. As an anecdote about how you can make use of this browser, I share a recent experience. I was about to attend a meeting (via a phone conference). The agenda was in my email, but just as I needed it, my computer decided that it needed to shut down suddenly. Rather than waiting for the slow rebooting and start up, I opened my NOOK Color's web browser, signed onto my email, tapped the attachment, and downloaded the file (a Word document) to My Downloads. I then opened the file with Quickoffice. I was using the agenda as the meeting was starting while my computer was still booting up.

CHAPTER 8

Using the Social Features of Your NOOK Color

As I'm sure you know, Facebook and Twitter are big deals these days—everyone is sharing everything. The NOOK Color makes this sharing even easier. You can share your reading status, share quotes, and rate and recommend books. You can share to specific contacts, on BN.com, Facebook, and Twitter. Because many of these options overlap and at the same time are scattered across the interface, this chapter focuses on Facebook sharing and the NOOK Friends app.

> NOTE: Although the locations for the sharing features are scattered, they make sense in their location. Basically, B&N provides many locations for the sharing features to make it easy to share.

> NOTE: For LendMe coverage, **see** Chapter 4, "Lending and Borrowing Books with LendMe on Your NOOK Color."
>
> Using Facebook and Twitter features requires that you link your Facebook and Twitter accounts to your NOOK Color. **See** Chapter 2's "Social Menu" section for linking your accounts.

> NOTE: The social features work only for NOOK Books and newspapers purchased from B&N. Only magazines purchased from B&N that function like newspapers (for example, *The New York Review of Books*) enable the social features.

You can access the Facebook social features by pressing and holding a cover image and tapping Recommend, tapping Recommend It on the View Details screen, tapping Share from the Reading Tools toolbar, or tapping Share from the Text Selection toolbar. Now deal with each of these contexts in turn.

Using Recommend from the Cover Menu or View Details Screen

Pressing and holding a cover either on the Home screen or in the Library displays a menu. Tap Recommend to see your recommend options (see Figure 8.1). Tap Facebook to see the Facebook Recommendation screen (see Figure 8.2)—if you are not currently connected to a Wi-Fi hotspot, the Network Setting screen appears for you to connect to one. Alternatively, you can press and hold a cover, tap View Details, and then tap Recommend It.

To post to your Facebook wall:

1. Tap Post to My Wall.

2. Type your message that will appear. As you type, you see the number of available characters (max of 420) go down, giving you an indication of how much space you have left.

3. Tap Post. Your NOOK Color sends the recommendation to your wall.

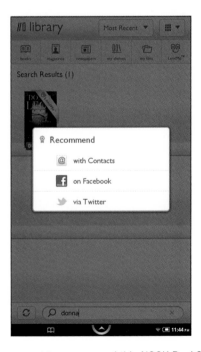

FIGURE 8.1   Where do you want to recommend this NOOK Book?

FIGURE 8.2   Use this screen to post a recommendation to your wall.

If you want to post to a friend's wall, tap Post to a Friend's Wall (see Figure 8.3) and then tap Select Friend. You can search for a name. To select a friend, tap the button on the right of the name. You can select however many friends you want. Tap Done. Type your message and then tap Post. Your NOOK Color sends the recommendation to your friend's or friends' walls.

> TIP: When you go to select friends, if you use the search box to narrow the list down, you may find that you now have a way to leave the screen. Actually, it's just hidden. Tap the hide keyboard key to get to the Done button.

FIGURE 8.3 Use this screen to post a recommendation to a friend's wall.

Using Share from the Reading Tools Toolbar

While reading a NOOK Book or newspaper, you can tap the Share button on the Reading Tools toolbar. You have three options: Recommend, Rate and Review, and Post Reading Status (see Figure 8.4).

▶ **Recommend**: This functions exactly as the previous section, "Using Recommend from the Cover Menu or View Details Screen," functions.

▶ **Rate and Review**: Tapping this allows you to rate and review the book on BN.com, which appears on the B&N book's specific web page. You must provide both a rating and either a headline or review before you can post. After you tap Post, the information is sent to BN.com.

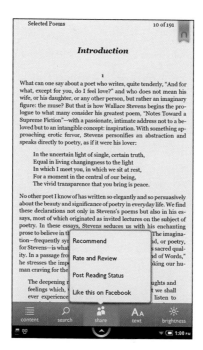

FIGURE 8.4   Tap the Share button to access the social features for NOOK Books.

▶ **Post Reading Status**: This option enables you to post how far along you are in reading this NOOK Book to Facebook. A brief headline indicating how far you are into the NOOK Book and its title is followed by the synopsis of the NOOK Book as found on BN.com.

After tapping Share and tapping Post Reading Status, tap the check box for Facebook or Twitter (or both) and then tap Post. The update is sent.

▶ **Like This on Facebook**: This option enables you to post to your Facebook wall that you like this book. Tap this link, and your NOOK Color makes the connection that you like that NOOK Book.

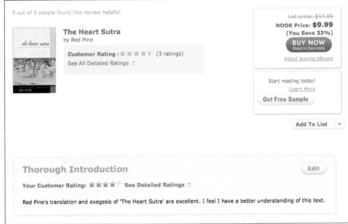

FIGURE 8.5   Rating and reviewing a NOOK Book posts that rating and review on BN.com.

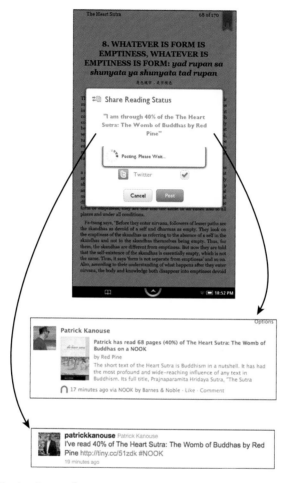

FIGURE 8.6 Sharing the reading status posts how far you are into that NOOK Book on Facebook and Twitter.

Using Share from the Text Selection Toolbar

Use this share function when you have a quote you want others to see:

1. Press and hold the word you want to start the quote.

2. When the Text Selection toolbar appears, finish highlighting the quote by dragging the ending blue bar to where you want.

3. Tap Share.

4. Tap Facebook (see Figure 8.7).

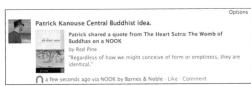

FIGURE 8.7 Sharing a quote.

5. Tap either Post to My Wall or Post to a Friend's Wall.

For Post to My Wall, type a message and tap Post.

For Post to a Friend's Wall, tap Select Friend. Select your friend or friends. Type your message. Tap Post.

The appropriate wall or walls are updated.

Using the Flag Reading Tools Bar

Remember the flag on the Reading Tools bar in the reading screen (that flag off to the right of the scroll bar). When you finish reading a NOOK Book, tap it to get access to more social functions. When you tap the flag, the We Hope You Enjoyed It screen appears (see Figure 8.8). You can rate and review it for BN.com, lend it to a friend (if it is a LendMe book), or recommend it to friends via your Contacts, Facebook, or Twitter.

FIGURE 8.8 What the Flag offers.

Also, if you click one of the covers in the Customers Who Bought This Also Bought section, the NOOK Store™ version Details screen appears so that you can buy your next NOOK Book, download a sample, or add it to your wishlist.

So What About Twitter and Contacts?

NOOK Color's support for Twitter and Contacts functions identically to Facebook, except that you share with specific contacts via email or your Twitter feed (see Figure 8.9). Twitter has a more limited character count, however.

FIGURE 8.9   Sharing a recommendation via Twitter.

> TIP: If you have a WordPress blog, check out the NOOK Color widget at http://wordpress.org/extend/plugins/nook-color-widget/. This widget displays the cover of book you are reading.

Using the NOOK Friends App

NOOK Friends is, to quote B&N, "the place for people who love to share their love for reading!" Here, you can connect with friends to lend and borrow books, see what your friends have been doing, and other things.

You access the NOOK Friends app by tapping Apps from the Quick Nav Bar. Then tap NOOK Friends. You are already set up with an account. The NOOK Friends screen is divided into Friends' Activities, NOOK Friends, LendMe, and About Me.

Friends' Activities displays what your friends have been reading, what they recommend, how far along they are in a book, and so on.

NOOK Friends displays the friends you have, any requests to become a NOOK Friend, and requests for NOOK Friends you have sent. If you tap the name of one of your friends, you see a screen that shows which of that person's books are available to borrow. Tap Requests when someone requests to be your NOOK Friend, which you can accept or decline. Tap Sent to see which NOOK Friends requests you have sent.

To send a request to become a NOOK Friend, tap the Plus button. The Add NOOK Friends screen appears (see Figure 8.10).

FIGURE 8.10   The Add NOOK Friends screen.

All Contacts displays to show all your contacts. Tap Invite to invite that contact, and she is sent an email and can see the request on her NOOK Color. Tap Suggested to see a filtered list of your contact that B&N knows already has a B&N account. You can also add a new contact by tapping Add New. Enter the person's first and last names and the email address. Leave the Invite as NOOK Friend check box marked to send that contact a request to become a NOOK Friend. Tap Save to send the request and save the contact.

Tap About Me to see information about you (see Figure 8.11).

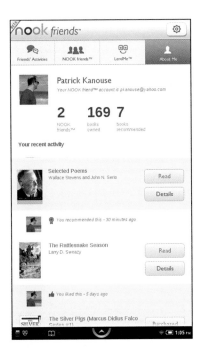

FIGURE 8.11   The NOOK Friends About Me screen.

This screen shows you the number of your NOOK Friends, NOOK Books owned, and NOOK Books recommended. You also see a list of your recent activity (and what your NOOK Friends see in their Friends' Activities screen).

The LendMe features are covered in Chapter 4's section, "Lending Using the NOOK Friends App."

CHAPTER 9

Shopping and Visiting B&N on Your NOOK Color

One of the greatest features of your NOOK Color is the capability to sample and buy content from B&N directly from the device. As long as you have a Wi-Fi connection, you can get new content for your NOOK Color no matter where you are. However, you can also use the B&N website to sample and purchase content for your NOOK Color.

> NOTE: Only customers with billing addresses in the Unites States, Canada, or a U.S. territory can order content from the B&N eBookstore. Citizens of U.S. territories are unable to preorder items.

Shopping on Your NOOK Color

To shop on your NOOK Color, from the Quick Nav Bar, tap Shop. Your NOOK Color displays the NOOK Store Home screen (see Figure 9.1).

Navigating the NOOK Store

The NOOK Store is divided into three parts. The top half features several constituent categories that you navigate by swiping left or right. The categories include the following:

- ▶ B&N Recommends
- ▶ Expand Your Mind and Your Horizons
- ▶ Explore History's Most Interesting Figures
- ▶ Edward's Picks (Biographies)
- ▶ Calling All History Buffs
- ▶ Stay in Step with the World
- ▶ Sessalee's Picks
- ▶ Jule's Picks (Mysteries)
- ▶ NOOK Apps
- ▶ Fall into This Season's Biggest Blockbusters

FIGURE 9.1   The opening of the NOOK Store.

NOTE: Yours may differ, but the general gist is that B&N features books that you might be interested in.

If you are interested in an ebook or app, tap the cover to see the Details screen.

The bottom half is mostly dominated by categories based on your buying patterns, Picked Just for You, along with fast-selling items, bargains, and new releases. Similarly, tap the cover to see the Details screen.

The bottom has a Browse button and a Search box. Type into the search box key-words, authors, titles—what have you. A list of titles appears. You can tap the cover to see the Details screen and tap the price to purchase the ebook (followed by a Confirm button). You can sort the list by Top Matches, Best Selling, Title, Price, and Release Date. Also, you can view them in one of three ways, similar to the Library view options: Grid, Large Cover List, and Small Cover List.

Browsing the NOOK Store

Tap the Browse button to see a variety of ways you can stroll through the available content (see Figure 9.2). The section is self-explanatory, so a lot of details here explaining the categories isn't necessary.

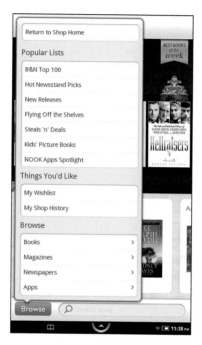

FIGURE 9.2 Browsing the NOOK Store.

The Popular Lists categories take you to specific lists of books. You can view in Grid, Large Cover List, and Small Cover List views. Additionally, tap the cover to see the Details screen, or tap the price to buy.

The Browse section functions like a narrowing list. Tap Books and you can see a host of sections. Tap a section to narrow this further. And this may run several more deep. You'll recognize your view options.

In the Things You'd Like section, the My Shop History brings up things you have sampled, looked up, and bought. The My Wishlist option shows your wishlist. Please note, that this wishlist is *not* the same as your BN.com wishlist. At this time, the two are separate.

> TIP: Myself? I dislike managing multiple wishlists. So I use the NOOK Color's browser to add to my B&N wishlist via the BN.com website. I use the Shop feature for its ease of use.

Sampling and Buying Content

After you locate and select an item you're interested in, if you tap the cover to get to the Details screen (see Figure 9.3), you see an overview page that describes the item and shows the rating of the item from other B&N readers. In addition, you see the following options:

- **Add to Wishlist**: Adds the item to your NOOK Color's wishlist.

- **Recommend It**: Gives you the opportunity to recommend the title. **See** Chapter 8, "Using the Social Features of Your NOOK Color," for more information.

- **Overview**: The default view displayed when you select an item.

- **Customer Reviews**: Displays reviews from other B&N customers. The number of reviews presented is likely to be smaller than the number of ratings.

- **Editorial Reviews**: Displays editorial reviews for the item. This view often shows details from the publisher along with critic reviews of the item. It can span multiple pages.

- **Screen Shots**: Displays screen shots for apps to give you an idea of what they look like.

- **More Like This**: Displays similar titles that you might be interested in. Tap the cover to jump to that ebook's Details screen.

If you like what you see, you can download a sample to your NOOK Color by tapping Free Sample. (Sampling is valid only with NOOK Books.) Samples typically consist of the first chapter of an ebook. However, it's up to the publisher to decide what to provide as a sample. In some cases, samples might contain just a few pages. In other cases, samples consist primarily of front matter, such as the title page, table of contents, dedication, and so on. One sample I downloaded contained nine pages of front matter and two pages of actual manuscript—hardly enough to get a feel for the book.

> NOTE: Samples never expire. You can keep a sample for as long as you'd like.

FIGURE 9.3 The Details screen in the NOOK Store.

If you decide to buy a book after reading the sample, simply go to the Details screen by tapping the cover (you can do this in the NOOK Store, on your Home screen, or in the Library) or tapping Buy Now in the reading screen of the sample. Because samples and full NOOK Books are completely separate products, a purchased book will not open at the point where the sample ended. You need to manually navigate to the point where you stopped reading the sample.

> NOTE: If a B&N gift card is associated with your account, the cost for items purchased from the B&N NOOK Store are applied against that gift card. If there is not enough credit left on the card, B&N charges the remaining balance to your credit card on file.

If you want to remove a sample from your NOOK Color, you need to visit My NOOK Library at bn.com from your computer. There is currently no way to remove a sample from your NOOK Color without using your computer to do so. If you delete a sample unintentionally, you can download it again.

For more information on using My NOOK Library, **see** Chapter 20, "Using My NOOK Library."

Is It Possible to Accidentally Purchase a Book You Have Already Purchased from B&N's eBookstore?

Your NOOK Color will not even present the option of purchasing a book you already own. If you select a book in the NOOK Store that you already own, you are shown an option to download or read the book, depending upon whether the book is already on your NOOK Color. However, you will not be shown an option to buy the book. It will read Purchased.

Some classic titles are released by multiple publishers. Two books of the same title from two different publishers are not considered the same title, so in these cases, you can purchase the same book twice.

Subscription content also enables sampling prior to purchasing, but it works a bit differently than it does with NOOK Books. When you subscribe to a newspaper or magazine, you are given a 14-day free trial (see Figure 9.4). If you cancel your subscription within that 14-day period, you will not be charged. If you cancel after the 14-day trial period, you will be refunded a prorated amount based on when you cancel.

FIGURE 9.4   The trial period for a magazine.

NOTE: You can buy the current issue by tapping Buy Current Issue without subscribing.

You can use a trial subscription only once for any particular item. For example, if you subscribe to *The Wall Street Journal* and cancel your subscription within the 14-day trial period, you will be charged beginning immediately if you were to subscribe to *The Wall Street Journal* again because you have already taken advantage of a trial subscription.

NOTE: Subscriptions can be canceled only using My NOOK Library at bn.com. You cannot cancel a subscription using your NOOK Color.

Your NOOK Color automatically downloads subscription content when it's available. In addition to seeing the new content in My B&N Library, you'll also receive notifications in The Daily for any new subscription content your NOOK Color downloads.

NOTE: You cannot sample NOOK Books for Kids that have Read to Me functionality.

Shopping on Your Computer

It's often easier and more convenient to shop for ebooks from your computer. Any books you purchase on your computer are added to My NOOK Library and are available for reading on your NOOK Color.

To shop for NOOK Books, magazines, and newspapers on your computer, browse to bn.com/ebooks. You can get samples of ebooks, subscribe to periodicals, and purchase books from the NOOK Store.

NOTE: You cannot shop for NOOK Apps at BN.com.

When you purchase, subscribe to a periodical, or choose to sample a NOOK Book from the online NOOK Book Store, the content is automatically added to your My NOOK Library. You can read the item on your NOOK Color or NOOK by opening connecting to Wi-Fi or Fast and Free Wireless. On your NOOK, you may need to tap Check for New B&N Content in B&N Library.

One of the great features of using the B&N website for browsing NOOK Books is that you can see which other formats are available. For example, if an MP3 audiobook is available for a title you're browsing, a link to the audiobook is there, so you can download it if you want.

When shopping for NOOK Books for kids, look for the "NOOK Kids Read to Me" statement in Format section. These NOOK Books have the Read to Me feature enabled. If the format for a NOOK Book for kids is simply NOOK Book, you will not have the Read to Me option for that NOOK Book for kids.

While shopping for NOOK Books, if you see that no NOOK Book is available for an in print book, on the product page for the print book, you see a link titled "Tell the publisher you want this in NOOK Book format." Click that link and you receive a message: "Thank you. We've notified the publisher that you'd like the book in ebook format." No guarantees, but at least the publisher will hear about it.

Whether you choose to shop from your NOOK or your computer, B&N provides plenty of great content for your NOOK at the NOOK Book Store. However, there are also plenty of other sources for great ebooks for your NOOK Color and NOOK. Some of those sources you can find in Appendix B, "Sources for ebooks Other than B&N," which you can then sideload to your NOOK Color or NOOK.

Using Your NOOK Color in a B&N Store

As mentioned earlier, B&N stores have a Wi-Fi hotspot so your NOOK Color can access free Wi-Fi while in the store (see Figure 9.5). B&N uses this hotspot to offer you special promotions called More in Store while in the store. Your NOOK Color automatically connects to a B&N hotspot when in the store, but you do need to ensure that Wi-Fi is turned on. (It's on by default.)

After your NOOK Color connects to the B&N hotspot, from the Quick Nav Bar, tap Shop.

In the top half of the NOOK Store, you see More in Store (see Figure 9.6). Generally, these offerings consist of several articles B&N feels might be interesting. Tap Read Free Content to see what's available. You are likely to find some interesting and others that don't interest you at all. If you'd like to get a sneak preview of what's available before you drive down to your local B&N, you can browse to http://www.barnesandnoble.com/=NOOK/moreinstore/ and see a list of all the More in Store offerings.

> NOTE: You need to be connected to the B&N hotspot to download and read the More in Store offerings.

FIGURE 9.5   The NOOK Color found the BN Wi-Fi hotspot.

FIGURE 9.6   The NOOK Store page that appears when you are in a B&N store.

When you're connected to a B&N hotspot in a B&N store, you have the ability to read any NOOK Book in the B&N store for up to an hour. Find a NOOK Book you'd like to read, tap the cover, the Details screen opens (see Figure 9.7). Tap the Read in Store button. The book opens. Read for up to an hour (see Figure 9.8).

> NOTE: Bookmarks, annotations, and highlights are not supported for Read in Store content.

If you read a bit of a book in the store, exit out of the book you were reading, get up for a cup of coffee, and decide you want to keep reading, at top the NOOK Store, tap the Recently Read in Store link. Tap the cover to see the Details screen.

FIGURE 9.7 Tap the Read in Store button to enjoy something to read on your NOOK Color while drinking a coffee.

FIGURE 9.8 The details for reading this book in store.

If you want to see what is available for reading in the store, go back to the main NOOK Store page, and swipe left in the top half until you get to the Read in Store page (see Figure 9.9). Tap Browse Read in Store eBooks.

There's no doubt that B&N has a unique opportunity because of its brick-and-mortar presence. No other ebook reader has the capability of being paired with a retail outlet, and there's every indication that B&N intends to beef up this feature in the future. It's certainly one of the more unique capabilities of the NOOK Color, and NOOK Color owners should be excited about what More in Store might offer in the future.

FIGURE 9.9   Browse for books to read in store.

NOTE: If you had the original NOOK, you know that you could show it to get a free cookie, coffee, smoothie, percentage off something, and more in the store. Currently, you can't get freebies or discounts with the NOOK Color.

CHAPTER 10

Rooting Your NOOK Color

At the beginning of this book, I mentioned that B&N used Google's Android operating system in your NOOK Color. Choosing Android makes business sense because it's an open-source operating system, and B&N didn't have to pay a small fortune to use it. However, the most exciting thing about Android for you is that it lets you easily root the NOOK Color and add new and exciting features.

The idea of rooting your NOOK Color may seem daunting or way too technical. However, I can assure you that rooting the NOOK Color to get basic Android Market apps installed is super easy, only requiring a bit of prep work and a few steps. This minimal effort (can be done inside a half-hour) is well worth the benefits, for you are turning your NOOK Color into a tablet (albeit without a microphone or camera), with access to the Android market amongst other benefits.

> NOTE: To complete the steps in this chapter, you must have at least a 2 GB microSD card.

> NOTE Rooting is another term for hacking, though without the illicit connotation of hacking.

An Introduction to Rooting Your NOOK Color

B&N locked down Android on your NOOK Color to prevent you from accessing some of Android's capabilities. However, by following a process called *rooting* your NOOK Color, you can open up these capabilities to make your NOOK Color more powerful and useful.

> NOTE: In the Android OS, *root* is the superuser who has access to everything in the OS. By rooting your NOOK Color, you can become the superuser on your NOOK Color.

Following are just a few of the things you can do after you root your NOOK Color:

- ▶ Add additional games.
- ▶ Use alternative browsers, PDF readers, and media players.
- ▶ Add calculator and note-taking apps.
- ▶ Access the Android Market.

These are just a few examples of the power unleashed by rooting your NOOK Color.

Before we go any further, I want to describe the various types of rooting available and the rooting method I will describe in this chapter. There are two types of rooting:

- ▶ **Internal Flash:** In this rooting method, you alter the memory on the NOOK Color itself. In other words, you alter the basic software on the NOOK Color.
- ▶ **microSD:** In this rooting method, you insert a microSD card in the NOOK Color and when you power up, the NOOK Color uses the microSD card to operate, thus leaving untouched the stock software on the NOOK Color.

I am going to show you the microSD rooting method. I am doing this for a few reasons:

- ▶ **Leaving the basic NOOK Color software intact**: One of the pros about using a microSD card root is that you do not void your warranty with B&N, and the likelihood of "bricking" your NOOK Color is nil.
- ▶ **Easy to swap between regular NOOK Color software and your root**: Want to read NOOK Books using the stock NOOK Color software? No problem. Power off. Remove the microSD card. Power on. You are now using the stock software. But wait, I want to use Evernote that I got at the Android Market. No problem. Power off. Insert the microSD card. Power on. You are now running a rooted NOOK Color.
- ▶ **B&N NOOK Color software updates**: Whenever B&N updates the software on the NOOK Color, you can update. If you use an Internal Flash rooting method, you have to wait for the people who develop the rooting methods to update their files. Consequently, you often have to reset your

NOOK Color to factory settings. Using the microSD card means you never have to reset to factory settings to use features beyond the NOOK Color.

The con of using the microSD card root is that the system can perform somewhat slower because it is running off the microSD card.

Is It Risky to Root My NOOK Color, and Does It Void My Warranty?

If you decided to use an Internal Flash rooting method, you root your NOOK Color using a process called *softrooting*, which involves installing a special software update for your NOOK Color. Therefore, rooting your NOOK Color is no more risky than installing a software update, and it's a completely reversible process.

With that said, rooting your NOOK Color is not sanctioned by B&N. Rooting is one of those things you must do at your own risk, and in my opinion, the benefits of using the microSD card rooting process are more than acceptable.

How to Root Your NOOK Color

The experts on rooting your NOOK Color all hang out at nookdevs.com and XDA-developers.com. Everything you need to know about rooting your NOOK Color, installing applications, and hacking the NOOK Color in general is available on these sites. All the files required to root your NOOK Color are freely downloadable from nookdevs or XDA-developers.com.

Froyo, Gingerbread, Honeycomb, What?

The NOOK Color originally released using Android OS version 2.1. This is also called Eclair.

Android OS Version	Name
2.0/2.1	Eclair
2.2	Froyo
2.3	Gingerbread
3.0	Honeycomb

The NOOK Color firmware update 1.2.0 upgraded the NOOK Color to Froyo, which supports Flash web pages among other things. Originally, many of the roots to the NOOK Color rooted using Froyo. But now that Froyo is the basic on the NOOK

Color, rooting to it seems less appealing. Honeycomb is only just released, and all the rooting options for it are considered experimental, so we will avoid it now.

We will be using a very stable root using Gingerbread, and this specific root uses CyanogenMod 7 (CM7).

Prerequisites

A few prerequisites before venturing down the path of rooting your NOOK Color. First and foremost, you obviously need to have a registered NOOK Color.

> CAUTION: If you do not register your NOOK Color with B&N prior to rooting, you will not be able to buy books from the NOOK Color's NOOK Bookstore™.

Second, you need a 2 GB or higher microSD card (I recommend using a 4 or 8 GB card). Any existing data on this card will be completely erased, so make sure you have it backed up. Third, you need a computer that can read that microSD card. Fourth, you need a working Wi-Fi connection for you NOOK Color. Finally, you need to have a Google account. You can get one from http://mail.google.com/mail/signup. You do not need to use it ever again, though you do need it for this process.

After you decide to experience the new functionality of your NOOK Color by rooting it, the steps required are quite easy:

1. Download the necessary files.

2. Create a disk image on a microSD card.

3. Install the microSD card disk image on your NOOK Color.

4. Enter some information into a couple of applications.

5. Install Android Market.

6. Install any additional applications you want on your NOOK Color.

Now look at each of these steps in detail.

> TIP: The steps I walk you through are documented at http://forum.xda-developers.com/showthread.php?t=1000957. However, there are a few points of possible confusion on that page, so although you can use it as a reference, follow my steps here for a successful rooting experience.

Download the Necessary Files

Now download the rooting files. You can find a single zip file at
http://patrickkanouse.blogspot.com/p/nook-book-updates.html. This zip file
contains several files:

- ▶ `generic-sdcard-v1.1.img.zip`. Unzip the file and place the `generic-sdcard-v1.1.img` file somewhere easily accessible.

- ▶ `update-cm-7.0.2-encore-signed.zip`. Do not unzip this file; rather, place it somewhere easily accessible.

- ▶ `gapps-gb-20110307-signed.zip`. Do not unzip this file; rather, place it somewhere easily accessible.

- ▶ `win32diskimager-RELEASE-0.1-r15-win32`. Unzip that file. Place the contents someplace easily accessible.

- ▶ `readme.txt`. Provides location to retrieve updated versions for the above files if necessary.

Create a Disk Image

In this step, you will create a bootable disk on the microSD card. To do this, you will
download some files, including a small piece of software (WinImager) that takes a
file and creates the bootable disk.

For Linux and Mac instructions for creating a disk image, see
http://nookdevs.com/NookColor_Rooting.

If you are on a PC:

1. Plug in a microSD card to your PC.

CAUTION: Following these steps will completely erase the microSD card, so
make sure you back it up to another drive.

---

2. Find the `win32DiskImage.exe` file you downloaded in the previous section.
   Double-click the file, which starts the program.

3. Browse to the `generic-sdcard-v1.1.img` file and select it.

4. For Device, choose the drive letter of the microSD card.

5. Click Write. The disk image will be created. When it finishes, click Exit.

6. Find the `update-cm-7.0.2-encore-signed.zip` file and copy it to the microSD card. The microSD card is now ready to install in your NOOK Color.

Rooting Your NOOK Color

CAUTION: Before you proceed any further, make sure that your NOOK Color has at least a 50% battery charge.

Now we are going to actually do the rooting process, which is strikingly easy. Follow these steps:

1. Unplug your NOOK Color from your computer and power it off.

2. Insert the microSD card you created a disk image on in the previous section into your NOOK Color.

3. Power on your NOOK Color.

4. You will see a penguin and then some green text. Let it do its thing.

5. After about a couple of minutes, you will see a notice that It Is Safe to Poweroff Now. Then the NOOK Color powers off.

6. You now have a rooted NOOK Color. Turn on your NOOK Color to finish this part of the rooting process. (You may need to hold the Power button longer than usual to get your NOOK Color to turn off.)

7. Once the NOOK Color is on, tap the Settings button in the far bottom left and then tap Settings. There are four buttons there: Settings, Back (a left-pointing arrow), Search (magnifying glass), and Quick Options (a circle with an upward-pointing arrow).

8. Tap Wireless & Networks.

9. Tap Wi-Fi Settings.

10. Tap your Wi-Fi network. (Enter a password if necessary.)

11. Use the Back button to get to the Settings. Tap Display.

12. Tap Screen Timeout and select a time. (The default is 1 minute.)

13. Turn off your NOOK Color to complete this part of the rooting process.

Finishing Rooting Your NOOK Color

You have only a few more steps to complete before you can begin to download Android Market apps and expand your NOOK Color into a tablet:

1. If your NOOK Color is on, turn it off.

2. Remove the microSD card.

3. Plug the microSD card into your computer.

4. Copy the `gapps-gb-20110307-signed.zip` to the microSD card.

CAUTION: Depending on your setup, you may or may not see the microSD card with two partitions as two drives. If you see this, one is called boot and the other is called CM7 SDCARD. Place the `gapps-gb-20110307-signed.zip` file in the boot partition.

---

5. You will see the following files on the microSD card:

   ▶ `gapps-gb-20110307-signed.zip`

   ▶ `MLO`

   ▶ `u-boot.bin`

   ▶ `uImage`

   ▶ `uRamdisk`

   ▶ `uRecImg`

   ▶ `uRecRam`

6. Change the file name `uImage` to `uImage.bak`.

7. Change the file name `uRamdisk` to `uRamdisk.bak`.

8. Change the file name `uRecImage` to `uImage`.

9. Change the file name `uRecRam` to `uRamdisk`.

10. Eject the microSD card from your computer.

11. Insert the microSD card into your NOOK Color.

12. Turn on your NOOK Color.

13. You will see a penguin and then some green text. Let it do its thing.

14. After a few seconds, you will see a notice that It Is Safe to Poweroff Now. Then the NOOK Color powers off.

15. Turn off your NOOK Color.

16. Remove the microSD card and plug it into your computer.

17. Change the file name uImage to uRecImage.

18. Change the file name uImage.bak to uImage.

19. Change the file name uRamdisk to uRecRam.

20. Change the file name uRamdisk.bak to uRamdisk.

21. Remove the microSD card from your computer and plug it into the NOOK Color.

22. Turn on the NOOK Color. The Backup and Restore screen appears.

23. If you want this device backed up with your Google Account, tap Finish Setup. If not, clear the checkbox and then tap Finish Setup.

24. Touch the Android.

25. Either create a Google account or tap Sign In to enter your Google account information.

25. Enter your Google account username and password and tap Sign In. A message titled Important: Read This! appears.

26. Tap OK. The Choose the Apps to Install screen appears.

27. Tap the checkboxes for the ones you want to install. Tap OK.

NOTE: You will have an opportunity to install other apps later.

---

28. Tap Accept.

28. For each of the apps you selected, tap the Free button and then the OK button.

30. Tap Finish Setup.

That's it! You have successfully rooted your NOOK Color!

Installing Applications on Your Rooted NOOK Color

Now that you have your NOOK Color rooted, you want to install applications, right? Well, it is super easy:

1. Tap the Apps button. (It's in between the Phone and Internet buttons.)

2. Tap the Market button. The Market page opens.

3. Tap the Search button. Type NOOK and tap Go.

4. Tap the NOOK for Android by B&N app line. Tap Free and then tap OK. You will be informed that it is downloading. Tap the Back button and then My Apps to watch the progress.

5. When it is finished downloading and installed, press the Home button.

6. Tap the Apps button.

7. Tap the NOOK button.

> TIP: To add an app to the Home screen, after tapping Apps, press and hold the app icon. You will be taken to the Home screen with the app there.

8. Enter your B&N account information. Your app is synched up with your B&N account. (If you have a large library, the synching can take some time.) You can now read your NOOK Books on the rooted portion of your NOOK Color.

Simple, right? And that's how installing other apps works. Check out what the Android Market has out there!

A Few Things to Note

Now that your have rooted your NOOK Color, you will want to keep a few things in mind:

▶ The NOOK Color does not have a GPS, camera, or microphone, so apps that use those features will not work. (For example, you cannot make calls with the Skype app—though you can IM.)

▶ Many of the references in the apps and market refer to your phone. This is quite natural for Android is widely deployed on phones. This terminology will change over time as more Android tablets (for example, the Samsung Galaxy) reach the market.

▶ The Return and Menu options change from app to app. The menu options in particular will provide access to settings, viewing options, etc.

Unrooting Your NOOK Color

Want to go back to stock NOOK Color software? Turn off your NOOK Color and remove the microSD card.

If you previously did an Internal Flash method of rooting, here are the steps for restoring the NOOK Color back to factory settings:

Part 1: Restart and Interrupt the Starting Process Eight Times

1. Turn off your NOOK Color.

2. Turn on your NOOK Color. Do not turn away.

3. When you see the "Welcome to the future of reading" screen, press and hold the Power button. This interrupts the start up process. If the Android start up animation does not appear, count 1 or add 1 to your start up count. If the Android start up animation appears, the restarting count is reset to 0, and you'll have to start over again.

4. Repeat the process from step 2 until you get up to 8 on the restart count.

5. The NOOK Color at this time flashes its firmware and you will see a screen that reads Installing, A New Software Update Is Being Installed. This Will Take a Few Minutes. Let the process finish.

Part 2: Reset the Device

1. With the NOOK Color off, hold the Home button and the Power button. The NOOK Color starts up. Keep holding the buttons.

2. You will see a screen to reset your NOOK Color to factory settings with two options. Press Power to exit. Press Home to continue.

3. Press the Home button. You will be given the two options again.

4. Press the Home button.

5. Your NOOK Color erases the data, deregisters, and reboots the device.

Your NOOK Color is no longer rooted.

CHAPTER 11

Getting Started with Your NOOK

Congratulations on your new NOOK. The NOOK second edition was released by B&N on June 4, 2011. This new NOOK features a touchscreen interface, removes the dual-screen of the first edition, and is smaller in size; reading on it is comfortable, though, and you won't notice any loss because of the size difference. Actually, the reading experience is significantly improved.

> NOTE: Barnes & Noble uses a lowercase *n* when it spells *NOOK* and for the NOOK's logo.

Before getting into the details of using your NOOK, you need to do some things right now.

Understanding NOOK Gestures

You control your NOOK, excepting the Power button, Home button, and page turn controls, with gestures:

- ▶ **Tap**: This is the most common gesture. Just press your finger to the screen and raise it. Usually you use this gesture with buttons and covers.

- ▶ **Double Tap**: This is the same as the Tap gesture, but just do it twice quickly.

- ▶ **Swipe Left/Swipe Right**: The gesture, mostly, for turning pages. Like a tap, touch your finger on the screen and quickly drag it to the left (or right) and lift your finger up.

- ▶ **Scroll**: Essentially the vertical version of the Swipe gesture. You can control the speed of the scroll by swiping up or down more rapidly. You can slow down or stop the scroll by tapping the screen (to stop) or pressing and holding to slow the scroll.

The NOOK Buttons

The NOOK features six physical buttons:

▶ **Power**: This does what it promises: turns your NOOK on or off. If you press it briefly while your NOOK is on, the NOOK goes to sleep. If the NOOK is asleep and you press it briefly, the NOOK wakes up.

▶ **Home**: The Home button (it's the lowercase n below the screen) shows you the Quick Nav Bar and is your way to change settings, go shopping, and so on. If you want to get back to a starting point, just press the Home button and tap Home.

If your NOOK is asleep, press this button to wake it up (and then drag your finger from left to right on the arrows at the bottom of the screen).

▶ **Page Turn**: These four buttons turn the page backward or forward and are alternatives to swiping left or right to turn the page. By default, the top buttons advance you forward one page and the bottom buttons take you backward in the book.

Registering Your NOOK

When you first turn on your NOOK, it asks you to register it to get started. The first step in getting started with your NOOK is to register it with Barnes & Noble (simply B&N from now on). To register your NOOK, you need an account on the B&N website. If you don't have one already, you can create one in the process of setting up your new NOOK.

> NOTE: B&N requires a default credit card with a valid billing address to be associated with your B&N account to register your NOOK.

Tap Next on the screen. You then see a screen with Terms and Conditions. Tap Agree if you agree to the terms. The next screen is the Time Zone screen. Tap the circle corresponding to your time zone and then tap Next.

The next part is to set up your Wi-Fi connection. (Or you can go into a B&N store where it has a connection you can connect to.) Your NOOK displays the available networks. Tap your network. If it is a secure network, enter the password and tap Done. Tap Continue with Setup.

On the Register Your NOOK screen, enter the email address and password you use to sign in to your account on the B&N website; then tap Sign In on the touchscreen. To move from the email field to the password field on the registration screen, tap in the Password field. If you need to create an account, tap Create Account and enter the required details.

You are then taken to the Get Started screen. You can tap Shop Now to begin shopping, tap Reader Guide to see the preloaded reader guide, or press the Home button to go to the Home screen.

> NOTE: If you live outside the United States and have trouble registering your NOOK, make sure you've upgraded to the latest firmware. As of version 1.2, B&N enables registration outside the United States.

For more information on connecting your NOOK to a Wi-Fi hotspot, **see** "Using Wi-Fi Hotspots," later in this chapter.

> NOTE: There's a great video walk-through showing how to register your NOOK at http://www.barnesandnoble.com/nook/support/index.asp?cds2Pid=35611.

Using Wi-Fi Hotspots

Your NOOK can also connect to other active Wi-Fi networks. B&N offers free Wi-Fi access in all B&N stores. If you take your NOOK to a B&N store, it automatically connects to the Wi-Fi hotspot in that store.

For more information on using your NOOK in a B&N store, **see** Chapter 17, "Shopping and Visiting B&N on Your NOOK."

To connect your NOOK to a Wi-Fi hotspot other than one in a B&N store, follow these steps:

1. Tap the Home button.

2. Tap Settings.

3. Tap Wireless. (If Wi-Fi is turned off, tap the Turn On Wi-Fi check box.)

4. Tap the Wi-Fi hotspot you want to use. (Your NOOK displays the SSID for all Wi-Fi hotspots in range.)

5. Tap Connect and enter the password for your Wi-Fi hotspot. (If you want to hide the password while typing, tap the Hide Password check box.) Enter a username or login name as well if required.

6. Tap Connect.

Your NOOK should now show that you are connected to your Wi-Fi hotspot on the reading screen. You should also see the Wi-Fi signal indicator at the top of the screen next to the battery indicator.

> NOTE: On the Home screen, you can tap the Wireless icon in the top bar. (Or tap just to the left of the batter.) Follow the preceding steps 2 through 6 to complete connecting to a Wi-Fi network.

If your Wi-Fi hotspot isn't listed after you tap Wi-Fi hotspot, tap Other hotspot. You can then enter the service set identifier (SSID), select the type of security (if the Wi-Fi is secured), and enter the password for your Wi-Fi hotspot if necessary. If you don't know this information, ask the person who set up the Wi-Fi network.

Your NOOK can connect to a Wi-Fi hotspot that requires you to browse to a web page to authenticate yourself. For example, many hotel Wi-Fi hotspots require you to enter a room number or other information to connect. When you tap this network name to connect to it, you are asked if you want to forget the network or continue on to a "redirect" to enter a password or other information. Tap Continue to continue the sign in procedure. (Your screen basically becomes a web page.)

Does My NOOK's Battery Drain Faster with Wi-Fi Connected?

I tested my NOOK's battery life with both Wi-Fi on and off. In my testing, the battery life was shorter when actively using Wi-Fi than it was when not. However, Wi-Fi affects battery life only when your NOOK is actually connected to a Wi-Fi hotspot. Simply having Wi-Fi turned on doesn't affect battery life.

Disconnecting from a Wi-Fi Hotspot

If you want to stop using a Wi-Fi hotspot, you need to disconnect your NOOK from the Wi-Fi hotspot. To do that, follow these steps:

1. Tap the Home button.

2. Tap Settings.

3. Tap Wireless.

4. To turn off Wi-Fi access completely, tap the Turn Off Wi-Fi check box. If you want to disconnect from a specific network, tap the name of the Wi-Fi hotspot you use. ("Connected" displays below the name of the Wi-Fi hotspot.)

5. Tap Forget to disconnect from the Wi-Fi hotspot.

For more information on configuring the settings in your NOOK (including turning off the Wi-Fi card), **see** "Your NOOK's Settings" in Chapter 12, "Customizing and Configuring Your NOOK."

Caring for Your NOOK's Battery

Your NOOK uses a high-tech battery called a lithium polymer battery. Unlike older rechargeable batteries, your NOOK's battery doesn't suffer from a charge "memory." However, you should still follow some basic rules to maximize the life of your battery:

▶ Try to avoid fully discharging your battery. Recharge it when it gets down to about 20% or so. Although charging it repeatedly is not necessarily a bad thing, the battery seems to function optimally if you charge it only when it drops down toward that 20% area.

▶ To maximize battery life, turn Wi-Fi off and leave it off. Turn on Wi-Fi to download your new books and subscription content and synch your reading across devices.

▶ Avoid high heat. Reading in sunlight is fine, but avoid storing your NOOK near a heat source.

▶ If storing your NOOK for a long period (a week or more), charge the battery to about 50% rather than giving it a full charge.

By following these steps, your NOOK's battery should last years.

Charging Your NOOK's Battery

You can charge your NOOK's battery either by plugging your NOOK into your computer's USB port or by plugging your NOOK into a wall outlet using the supplied AC adapter. Plugging your NOOK into a wall outlet is preferred because it charges the NOOK much more quickly.

Should I Plug My NOOK into a Surge Suppressor?

Just like any electronic device, your NOOK is susceptible to power spikes and other electrical anomalies. If you want to ensure that your NOOK is protected from electrical problems, plug it into a surge suppressor.

When You Are Not Reading

When you finish reading, let your NOOK go to sleep instead of turning it off. I realize that it's not intuitive to leave electronic devices turned on, but because your NOOK uses almost no power unless you do something that requires it to refresh the E Ink display, you can leave it turned on without draining your battery.

By leaving your NOOK on, it occasionally downloads content from B&N such as subscription content (assuming you have Airplane Mode turned off), updated information for The Daily (articles of interest to NOOKies), and any books that you purchase from the B&N website. When you're ready to start reading again, simply press and release the power switch at the top of your NOOK to wake it up.

How Should I Clean My NOOK's Touchscreen?

Your NOOK's touchscreen is going to get dirty and covered in fingerprints. The best way to clean it is to use a dry, microfiber cloth like the one you would use to clean eyeglasses. If you must use a cleaning fluid, spray it lightly on the cloth and then wipe the touchscreen. Use only cleaning sprays designed for cleaning LCD displays.

CHAPTER 12

Customizing and Configuring Your NOOK

Your NOOK has many features that enable you to easily customize it and make it your own, and many settings control how your NOOK operates. In this chapter, you examine how to customize and configure your NOOK.

Using Custom Screensavers

You can customize your NOOK by using custom screensaver images. Your NOOK displays screensaver images on the Reading screen when it is sleeping. Even though your NOOK's Reading screen isn't a color screen, it can display 16 levels of gray, making it ideal for displaying black-and-white versions of your favorite pictures.

Creating Screensaver Images

Before you use a picture as a screensaver on your NOOK, you need to resize it to fit the dimensions of your NOOK's Reading screen. Screensaver images should be 800 pixels high and 600 pixels wide. For information about creating wallpapers and screensavers, **see** Appendix D, "Using Picasa to Create Wallpapers and Screensavers."

> NOTE: You don't have to resize your images, but by doing so you can display them at their maximum size.

> **Should I Use a Specific File Format for Images?**
>
> Your NOOK supports JPEG (.JPG), GIF, and PNG files. For images, using either JPEG or PNG is your best option. GIF isn't a good option for photographs, but if your image is a line art or text, GIF can work fine. If you're unsure, stick with JPEG. That's what Picasa uses by default.

Copying Screensaver Images to Your NOOK

Screensavers on your NOOK consist of a series of images. Each time your NOOK sleeps, it displays the next image in the series on the reading screen. You select a specific set of images to use as a screensaver by placing them on your NOOK in a folder.

Copy screensaver images to your NOOK by following these steps:

1. Connect your NOOK to your computer with the USB cable. When you do, your NOOK appears in your computer as a new drive called NOOK.

2. If your computer doesn't automatically display the folders on your NOOK, open your NOOK via My Computer on Windows or the Finder on the Mac. You should see the Screensavers folder.

3. Open the Screensavers folder.

4. Create a new folder for your screensaver. The new folder's name is the name of your screensaver on your NOOK. Note that the folder name should not be two words: Vacation-Pictures is correct, but Vacation Pictures is incorrect.

5. Copy the image files for your screensaver into the folder you created in step 4.

For example, if you have a series of images of your summer vacation, you might want to create a new folder in the Screensavers folder called Vacation-Pictures and copy your images into that folder. You can then use the images in that folder as your screensaver by selecting Vacation-Pictures as your screensaver.

Now that you've copied your custom images to your NOOK, look at how you can change the settings on your NOOK to use the new images as your wallpaper or screensaver.

Choosing a Custom Screensaver

Your NOOK's Settings menu enables you to change the screensaver on your NOOK. Here's how:

1. Tap the Home button.

2. Tap Settings.

3. Tap Screen in the Settings menu.

4. To change the screensaver, tap Screensaver and select the folder name of your screensaver. The Authors and Nature screensaver folders are on the NOOK by default, and you cannot remove them.

Screensavers from Other Sources

You can use several online sources for NOOK screensavers. One of the best is
NOOK-Look (www.NOOK-look.com). NOOK-Look provides a wide assortment of
quality screensavers for your NOOK.

Another way you can locate screensavers for your NOOK is by using the image
search feature on your favorite search engine. A search for "NOOK screensavers" in
Google turns up plenty of images presized for your NOOK. The same search on Bing
is less helpful, but by clicking the Images of NOOK Screensaver link on the left of
the page, clicking the Images tab, and selecting Tall on the Layout menu, plenty of
images are available in the correct size for your NOOK.

One Step Further—Decals

If you want to take the ultimate step to customize your NOOK, a DecalGirl skin
(www.decalgirl.com) is the perfect addition. DecalGirl skins are vinyl skins with
adhesive backing that you can easily apply. Many skins also include matching NOOK
wallpaper that provides a truly unique look.

Your NOOK's Settings

Your NOOK offers configurable settings for controlling many of its features. Tap the
Home button and then tap Settings to access the Settings menu. Your NOOK displays
the following information in the Settings menu.

Device Info

The Device Info section displays a variety of information about your NOOK:

- ▶ **Battery**: Displays how charged your battery is and whether it is charging or
  discharging.

- ▶ **Available Storage**: Shows how much free space you have on the internal
  memory of the NOOK. Your NOOK has 2GB of storage space (although
  B&N reserves 750MB of that for B&N-specific storage.)

- ▶ **SD Card**: Shows whether you have a microSD card installed. See "Adding a
  microSD Card to Your NOOK" for more about microSD cards.

- ▶ **About Your Nook**: Shows the personal information related to your NOOK:
  Owner name, account to which this NOOK is associated, software (also
  called firmware) version, and such.

The Software section displays the version of software (called *firmware*) currently installed on your NOOK. B&N releases periodic updates to the NOOK to improve performance and fix known issues. As long as your NOOK has a connection to a Wi-Fi connection, your NOOK automatically downloads any updates that B&N releases.

Not all NOOK owners receive new firmware updates at the same time. B&N rolls out new firmware over a period of about a week. If you would like to update your NOOK manually, you can visit http://www.barnesandnoble.com/u/nook-support-software-updates where B&N typically provides instructions for manually updating your NOOK to the latest firmware.

If I Don't Like Changes Made by a Firmware Update, Can I Go Back to an Older Version?

On some sites, you can download older versions of NOOK firmware (www.NOOKdevs.com), but because your NOOK automatically installs firmware updates when B&N makes one available, your NOOK will always install the latest update unless you keep Wi-Fi turned off.

▶ **Erase & Deregister Device**: Enables you to erase all content from and deregister the device. This action resets the NOOK to factory defaults, something you should consider doing if you are going to give your NOOK to someone else. B&N technical support also might ask you to reset your NOOK during troubleshooting. However, outside of those reasons, you likely won't ever need to reset it.

CAUTION: Resetting your NOOK to factory defaults removes all content from its internal memory. Content stored on a microSD card is not removed. Before you reset it to factory defaults, make sure you have backups of any personal documents stored in your NOOK's internal memory.

Wireless

This setting enables you to turn on or off Wi-Fi access and set up connections to Wi-Fi networks. **See** the section "Using Wi-Fi Hotspots" in Chapter 11, "Getting Started with Your NOOK," for more information about Wi-Fi hotspots.

TIP: If you travel on a flight that offers Wi-Fi service and you want to use the hotspot with your NOOK, turn off Wi-Fi access. When aboard and cleared to turn on electronic devices, turn on Wi-Fi access and select the airplane's network. However, check with the flight crew first to avoid any problems.

Screen

Here you can alter the screen timeout length and change screensavers.

The Screen timeout option controls the time interval after which your NOOK puts itself to sleep. This timer is set to 5 minutes by default. To change the interval, tap Screen Timeout, and then tap the desired time interval.

TIP: If you set the sleep timer to a time interval shorter than the amount of time it takes you to read a page on the reading screen, your NOOK goes into sleep mode while you are reading. So, be sure you set the interval appropriately for your reading speed.

Because your NOOK uses almost no battery power when you read, 10 minutes is likely a suitable interval for most people.

Time

These settings enable you to select your current local time zone and select a 12-hour or 24-hour clock format.

Reader

This option enables you adjust the set up the physical page control buttons. By default, the top buttons advance you forward in a book. But if you want the bottom buttons to advance you forward in a book, tap the Open button just above Page Forward with Bottom Buttons.

Shop

This option enables you set up some basic shopping features when shopping from your NOOK:

- ▶ Require Password for Purchases enables you to require to have the password entered for any purchases.

▶ Clear Wishlist and Clear Recently Viewed Lists do just what they say they do. The wishlist on the NOOK is not connected to any other NOOK or NOOK Color devices or to your BN.com wishlist, so clearing the wishlist does it for this NOOK only.

Social

This option contains several screens for configuring your NOOK's Social settings, for which you will need to have an active Wi-Fi connection. Basically, you can link your Facebook and Twitter accounts and Google Contacts lists to this NOOK, which enables you to share quotes and recommendations directly to your and your friends' Facebook walls and Twitter account.

> TIP: If you have earlier set up your Facebook, Twitter, and Google Contacts info (for example, you have a NOOK Color) for this username, your NOOK automatically sets up your Facebook, Twitter, and Google Contacts information.

▶ Tap Link to Facebook, Twitter, and Google to access these specific settings. If you have already linked your Facebook account, you can unlink it. To link it, tap Link Your Account. Then enter the required information and tap Log In. You'll be asked to allow Facebook and your NOOK to share information. Tap Allow. For more information about Facebook with your NOOK, **see** Chapter 16, "Using the Social Features of Your NOOK."

For Twitter, if you have already linked your Twitter account, you can unlink it. To link it, tap Link Your Account. Then enter the required information and tap Sign In. Twitter asks you to allow this linking to occur. Tap Allow to do so. For more information about Twitter with your NOOK, **see** Chapter 16.

Google Contacts: This enables you to link your Google Contacts list to this NOOK. If you have already linked your Google Contacts list, you can unlink it. To link it, tap Link Your Account. Then enter the required information. If you want the NOOK to remember this information should you come back to this screen, tap the Remember Me check box; then tap Go. Google wants to know if you want to grant access to the NOOK to do this linking. Tap Grant Access to do so.

▶ Manage My Contacts: This enables you to add and edit your NOOK contacts list (for example, if you don't use Google Contacts, you can just use contacts on your NOOK). When you tap this, you see a list of your contacts.

From the drop-down list, you can choose to see only your NOOK Friends or Google Contacts. The default is to see all of your contacts. To see the details for your contacts, tap the contact's name. If the contact is not a NOOK Friend, you can tap the checkbox Invite as a NOOK Friend and tap Send to invite that person. Tap View Emails to see all the email addresses. If the contact is not a Google Contact or NOOK Friend and is one you added directly to the NOOK, you can tap Modify to adjust the contact's information. Those are the only contacts you can delete as well (tap Modify and then tap Delete This Contact). To update Google Contacts, log in to your Google account on your computer and update.

Search

This option enables you to clear recent searches you have made on your NOOK. For example, if you have searched for "poetry" in your library, that appears when you go to do a new search in your library. If you want to clear those historical searches, tap Clear Recent NOOK Searches.

Adding a microSD Card to Your NOOK

Your NOOK has approximately 1.3GB of built-in usable memory. That's enough memory for an enormous library of books. However, it might not be enough memory if you add pictures and even more books to your NOOK. Therefore, your NOOK's memory is expandable using a microSD card.

> TIP: A microSD card is not the same as an SD memory card like the kind typically used in digital cameras. A microSD card is approximately the size of your fingernail.

To install a microSD card, you need to open the flap on the top right of your NOOK.

1. The microSD slot is the small opening. With the metal connectors of the microSD card facing the front of the NOOK, slide the microSD card in, and push until it locks into place. The NOOK automatically recognizes the card, and you hear a beep. Close the metal plate.

2. If the microSD card has not yet been formatted, a screen appears letting you know that formatting it will erase everything on the disk. Tap Format Now. Tap Format Now again to confirm.

On the Device Info screen (from the Quick Nav Bar, tap Settings, and then tap Device Info), tap SD Card (only available to tap if a microSD card is installed). This opens the SD Card screen. Here, you can see information related to the amount of free memory available on the microSD card.

Tap Unmount SD card if you want to remove or format the microSD card. The card unmounts, and you can follow the preceding step 1 to remove. (Just press the card in farther and it pops out.)

If you tap Format SD Card, you can format the microSD card, which erases everything on the card. (This option is only available after tapping Unmount SD Card.) A confirmation screen to format and erase all data on the micro SD card appears. Tap Format to do so. Tap OK when done.

When you connect your NOOK to your computer, you now see your microSD card in addition to your NOOK's built-in memory. (It is the drive called NO NAME.)

> NOTE: You can add a microSD card that already has items loaded on it, but the NOOK folder structure is necessary, so it is easiest to install a blank microSD card into the NOOK and then plug the NOOK into your computer and load files into the appropriate categories (documents, videos, and so on).

Now that you have a microSD card installed, how do you access those files? From the Quick Nav Bar, tap Library and then tap My Files from the type drop-down list (the far left drop-down list beneath Library).

Can I Use a High-Capacity microSD Card in My NOOK?
Yes. The NOOK supports microSDHC cards up to 32 GB.

CHAPTER 13

Reading on Your NOOK and Beyond

Although your NOOK has many unique features and capabilities, when it comes right down to it, its primary purpose is for reading books and other content. One of the benefits of owning a NOOK is that you can carry a complete library with you everywhere you go. If you don't happen to have your NOOK with you, you can also read your ebooks on your PC, Mac, iPhone, iPad, iPod touch, Android phone, and Blackberry.

Various forms of content are available to read on your NOOK, such as NOOK Books, PDFs, and other EPUB ebooks. Appendix A, "Understanding ebook Formats," explains more about the details of ebook formats.

Can I Read Word Documents or TXT Files on My NOOK?

If you want to read Word documents or TXT files on your NOOK, you need to first convert them into a format compatible with your NOOK.

Calibre can convert TXT files to the EPUB format for your NOOK. If you want to read a Word document, you should save the file as a PDF file. (Recent versions of Word provide this functionality.) If you cannot save the Word document as a PDF, first save it as an HTML file, and then use Calibre to convert it for your NOOK.

For more information on using Calibre to convert ebooks, **see** Chapter 19, "Managing Your ebooks with Calibre."

Browsing Your Library

There are two main places for content on your NOOK: The Home screen and My Library.

The Home Screen

The Home screen includes information automatically delivered to your NOOK in the New Reads section, which includes new subscription content, new samples, and new ebooks. Tap See Library at the bottom of the New Reads section to go to your full library.

TIP: Some notifications such as new subscription content and LendMe offers show up as balloon tips in the top information bar on your NOOK's Home screen. You can access more details on these notifications by tapping the balloon.

The Reading Now section shows the last item you were reading along with which page you are on. Tap the cover to continue reading that content.

Additionally on the Home screen, B&N provides recommendations for what to read next at the bottom of the screen. These picks are based on your purchase history. Tap a cover to see more details about that NOOK Book, including an option to purchase it. Tap See All B&N Picks to connect to the B&N store. **See** Chapter 16, "Using the Social Features of Your NOOK," to learn more about shopping on your NOOK.

The Library

The Library contains all the content you purchase from B&N. This includes not only books you purchase, but also magazine and newspaper subscriptions, sample books, free books downloaded from B&N, documents you place on the NOOK, and everything else.

First, consider the basic controls in the Library:

- ▶ **Synch (button is two arrows forming a circle)**: The Synch button forces your Library to update, which means that it downloads any new content that has not yet downloaded and synchs reading location, annotation, notes, and bookmarks on NOOK Books across NOOK reading devices (NOOK Color, NOOK, NOOK for iPad, and so on).

- ▶ **Search (button is a magnifying glass)**: Tap this to search your Library. When the search screen appears, type your search criteria and tap the Search key. You can scroll through the results (if more than a few). Tap the item to open it. Tap Close to close the search screen and return to the Library. This feature doesn't search inside your content. It searches only the *metadata* for your content. Metadata includes the title, author, publisher, contributors, and subject.

- ▶ **Type**: The default is All, but you can narrow what you see in your Library by choosing what type of content you want to see: All, Books, Newsstand, LendMe, Shelves, My Files, Archived, or Everything Else.

NOTE: Here "All" doesn't really mean "all." All shows all content except for Archived and Everything Else items. However, when you narrow your choice to see only Books, Newsstand, or LendMe, archived content also appears.

To change what you want to see, tap the drop-down list, and then tap your choice. A few of them offer additional actions beyond seeing what's available. Newsstand items show the overall subscription with the number of issues available. Tap the cover to see the individual issues. Tap the individual issue's cover to open it.

LendMe shows your NOOK Books available to Lend.

Shelves enables you to see any shelves you created and enables you to add more. **See** "Shelves" for more information about using them.

My Documents enables you navigate the NOOK internal memory and the microSD card for non-NOOK Books content. Tap the folder to navigate to the location you want, and then double-tap the file to open it.

In Archived, tap the Unarchive button on the cover (or to the right of the title's name) to unarchive the title.

▶ **Sort**: Enables you to sort what you are viewing by the Most Recent items (that is, added to the NOOK), by title, or by author.

▶ **Grid/List View**: These two options (Grid view is a set of nine boxes in a grid format, whereas List view is a set of five stacked lines) determine how you view the content in the Library. Grid shows the covers. List shows the title without the cover.

▶ **Library**: This is, of course, the main reason for this screen. You can scroll through the Library. Double-tap the cover (or the title if in List view) to see the Title Details screen. **See** "View Item Details & Options" for more information about that screen. Tap the cover (or the title if in List view) to open that ebook.

Items in the Library are in one of three categories:

▶ **Items on your NOOK**: Items on your NOOK are available for reading immediately by selecting the item. They are stored in your NOOK's memory or on a microSD card if one is installed.

▶ **Archived items**: These are items in My NOOK Library on bn.com and that have been downloaded to your NOOK at one point but that have since been removed from your NOOK. These items appear as light-colored text (grayed out) in the Library.

▶ **Everything Else**: These are items in My NOOK Library that are not compatible with the NOOK. For example, the NOOK Color supports apps, but the NOOK does not. So the Library shows any apps you have purchased. Other examples include NOOK Books for Kids, some magazines (for example, National Geographic), and textbooks among others.

For more information on using My NOOK Library on bn.com, **see** Chapter 20, "Using My NOOK Library."

When you purchase a NOOK Book, that book is added to My NOOK Library on bn.com and is downloaded to your NOOK.

CAUTION: If you plan to be away from Wi-Fi hotspots, you should make sure that the items that appear in the Library have actually been downloaded to your NOOK.

Some items in the Library might have an indicator banner on the top-right corner of the cover or to the right of the title. This icon indicates special properties of the item (such as the ability to lend the item to a friend using the LendMe feature), or it might indicate that an item has been lent to someone or is borrowed from someone.

For more information on the LendMe feature, **see** Chapter 14, "Lending and Borrowing Books on Your NOOK Using LendMe."

The following icons might be displayed for an item:

▶ **LendMe**: Indicates that the item can be lent to a friend using the LendMe feature.

▶ **On Loan**: Indicates that the item has been lent to a friend. You cannot read this item for a period of 14 days from the lend date.

▶ **Borrowed**: Indicates that the item has been borrowed from a friend. The item will be available to you for 14 days.

▶ **Lent to You**: Indicates that the item is one that a friend has offered to lend to you. After you accept the offer, the item shows a Borrowed banner.

▶ **Sample**: Indicates that the item is a sample ebook from B&N.

▶ **Returned**: Indicates that a NOOK Book you borrowed has been returned.

You can also see the buttons Download and Unarchive on the cover in Grid view (or the right of the title in List view). Tap Download to download the NOOK Book from B&N. Tap Unarchive to unarchive the book.

View Item Details & Options

When you double-tap a cover in the Library, you see the Title Details screen. The available options differ depending on the content you select:

- ▶ **Download**: Displayed only when the content has not already been downloaded to your NOOK. Tapping Download transfers it using Wi-Fi.

- ▶ **Read**: Displayed only when the content has been downloaded to your NOOK. Tapping Read opens the content on the reading screen.

- ▶ **LendMe**: Displayed only when the publisher has enabled the LendMe feature. This menu item enables you to lend the content to a friend.

- ▶ **Rating**: A series of stars is available so that you can rate your content. Tap the stars, and five large stars display. Touch the star that corresponds to your rating.

> TIP: If you want to remove your rating, tap the leftmost star, and drag your finger toward the left away from the stars.

- ▶ **Overview**: This displays a description of the item (if available) and other details.

- ▶ **Reviews**: For B&N content, you can see customer and editorial reviews of that NOOK Book. You can also add a review. **See** Chapter 16 for more information.

- ▶ **Related Titles**: This displays similar titles divided by either Those Who Bought This Book Also Bought These Others or Other Books by the Author.

- ▶ **Share**: For more information about this feature, **see** Chapter 16.

- ▶ **Archive**: Removes the selected content from your NOOK's storage. The item is still visible in the Library, but if you want to read the content, you need to unarchive it first.

> NOTE: There isn't a way to delete content from your library from the NOOK. To delete content (including sample books), you need to use My NOOK Library at the B&N website.

For more information on using My NOOK Library, **see** Chapter 20.

Shelves

You can organize your ebooks into shelves, aligning them into whatever categories you want for easier access to similar ebooks. You can go directly to a shelf of books by pressing the Home button, tapping Library, and tapping Shelves in the Type list. If you have more than four titles on the shelf, tap See All to see all the titles on that shelf.

If you have shelves you created and you want to place ebooks onto those shelves, tap Edit. A list of title appears. Scroll to the title or titles you want, tapping the check box along the way. Tap Save to add those titles to the shelf. If you want to remove titles from the shelf, simply tap the check box to clear out the check box, and tap Save. You can add and remove titles at the same time.

The Sort options for shelves changes to Most Recent and Shelf name. Just tap the Sort drop-down list, and tap the sort order you want.

To create a new shelf, from the Shelf screen tap Add Shelf. Type the name of the shelf and tap Save. Add titles. (Although this is not required.) Tap Save.

To remove a shelf, tap Edit for the Shelf you want to delete, tap Delete Shelf, and tap OK.

To rename a shelf, tap Edit for the Shelf you want to delete, tap Rename, update the name, and tap Save.

Archiving Library Items

As mentioned earlier, you can archive an item by double-tapping the cover and then tapping Archive in the Overview tab. Archiving is a means to remove an item you purchased from B&N from your NOOK. Archived items still display in the Library, but they display with the Unarchive banner.

When an item is archived, you can still view details on the item, rate the item, and lend the item to a friend using the LendMe feature. However, to read the item, you must unarchive it.

To unarchive an item, tap Unarchive on the cover. The item begins downloading and disappears out of the Archived view.

> TIP: You can manage your ebook library (including archiving and unarchiving items) using My NOOK Library at bn.com. My NOOK Library is covered in detail in Chapter 20.

My Files

My Files contains content you manually copy to your NOOK from other sources. B&N calls the process of manually copying books and other content to your NOOK *sideloading*, and any reading content you sideload onto your NOOK appears in the My Files portion of the Library (and also when you view All content).

> TIP: If you view the Library, you can switch to My Files by tapping My Files from the Type drop-down list.

View Item Details & Options

When you double-tap a My Files cover, you see the details for the selected item. Details include the publisher, publication date, and so on if available. You also see the file path for the selected item.

> TIP: The file path begins with my media if the selected item is stored in your NOOK's internal memory. If the item is stored in a microSD card, it begins with sdcard.

You have only one option from this Details screen: Open.

> **How Can I Delete Sideloaded Content Because There Isn't a Menu Option to Remove It?**
>
> Sideloaded content must be deleted by connecting your NOOK to your computer and removing the content. The easiest way to manage your sideloaded content is to use Calibre, a free ebook management application. **See** Chapter 19.

Reading Books on Your NOOK

If you open a NOOK Book or sideloaded EPUB file for the first time, after you select it, you go to the starting point that the publisher chose for that item. This might or might not be the first page. For example, this ebook opens on the first page of Chapter 1, "Getting Started with Your NOOK Color." Other ebooks open on the cover or title page. The publisher of the book decides which page is visible when you first open an ebook.

If you open a NOOK Book that you have read on the NOOK before in any of the NOOK Apps, NOOK Study, or NOOK Color, you are taken to the last location you were reading. If you open a sideloaded EPUB file you have read on the NOOK before, it opens to the last page you were on in the NOOK. In other words, non-B&N content does not sync across applications.

As you're reading, swipe right across the page to go to the previous page or swipe left across the page to go to the next page or use the buttons to the left and right.

Of course, there's more to reading books than just reading, right? To see the Reading Tools, quickly tap the reading screen. (B&N recommends tapping the middle of the screen.)

The following are the Reading Tools options:

- **Content**: This opens up a screen to navigate the table of contents, notes and highlights, and bookmarks. To go to a specific table of contents, note, high-light, or bookmark, simply tap the appropriate tab, and tap the table of content location you want to go to. **See** Chapter 15, "Using Highlights, Bookmarks, and Annotations," for more details about using these features.

- **Find**: Tap this option to search the text within this book. Type the text and tap Search. The NOOK searches through the book and displays the results, providing the page number and some context for the search word. If you want to go to the location of that search, tap the row and you are taken there. Otherwise, tap Close.

> TIP: Typing lots of uppercase letters? Tap the Shift key twice. (It has a white highlight around the key.) This enables you to enter only uppercase letters. Tap the Shift key again to release the Caps Lock.

- **Go To**: Tapping this displays a scrollbar, your location within the book, and two options: Go Back and Go to Page. To scroll to a specific page, tap the vertical bar, and drag it to the location you want to go to. As you scroll the page number and location information change to reflect that location. To go to a specific page, tap Go to Page, type the number of the page, and tap Go. In either case of scrolling or going to a specific page, if you want to go back to the position in the book you were at immediately prior, tap Go Back.

- **Text**: Tap this to access the font and size options. See "Changing the Text Font and Text Size" section for more details.

- **More**: This opens up the Details screen.

To exit the Reading Tools, tap anywhere on the reading screen without those tools appearing.

Finally, while reading, you can press and hold on a word. The Text Selection Toolbar appears. If you want to select more than that single word, drag the selection highlight to the end of the block of text you want to select. For the Highlight, Add Note, and Look Up buttons, **see** Chapter 15. For the Share button, **see** Chapter 16. The "Looking Up Words" section discusses looking up words.

Changing the Text Font and Text Size

Your NOOK enables you to easily change the text font and text size while you read.

The text options are available from the Text option on the Reading Tools screen. An array of options display: Size, Font, Line Spacing, Margins, and Publisher Defaults. (If the options are locked down by the publisher, you may only have an option to adjust the text size.)

Your NOOK supports seven text sizes, represented by the A. The current text size A is black, whereas the sizes not used are gray. (Additionally, a small arrow appears above the size in use.) Tap the A for the size you want. You can see the text size adjust behind the text menu. Adjust the text size to whichever size you want.

The current font used has an arrow next to it. To change the font, tap from the six available fonts.

▶ You cannot change the text font if the publisher created the content with a specific font embedded in it.

▶ You cannot change the text font for PDF files. If the creator of the PDF file embedded a particular font, your NOOK uses that font. Otherwise, it uses the default font.

▶ Some ebooks consist of pages scanned as images, usually as PDF files. You cannot change the text font for these ebooks.

> NOTE: Tapping Publisher Defaults to On changes all settings on this screen to the options chosen by the Publisher for all content that you read. You can toggle that back to Off at any time.

The Line Spacing options are similar to using single space or double space. The current selection is the darker option and has an arrow above it. You have three options. Tap the option you want. The reading screen adjusts.

The Margin options determine the amount of white space on the right and left sides of the text. The current selection is the darker option and has an arrow above it. You have three options. Tap the option you want. The reading screen adjusts.

Looking Up Words

One of the most convenient features of your NOOK is to quickly look up the definitions of words you don't know. If you're reading a book and encounter a word you don't know or are curious about, press and hold on that word until the Text Selection toolbar appears. Tap Look Up. A window appears with a dictionary entry.

> NOTE: Looking up words is not supported for certain types of ebooks—for example, ADE PDFs and PDFs.

Reading Magazines and Newspapers on Your NOOK

In addition to books, B&N provides magazine and newspaper subscriptions for your NOOK. B&N automatically delivers subscription content to your NOOK if a Wi-Fi connection is available.

For more information on subscribing to content on your NOOK, **see** Chapter 17, "Shopping and Visiting B&N on Your NOOK." Some magazines are not supported for reading on your NOOK (for example, *National Geographic*), so be sure to check the supported NOOK devices and apps on the B&N website.

Unlike books, magazine and newspaper content isn't presented in a linear format. Content is often presented as article headlines followed by a small synopsis of each article. To read the specific article, tap the headline for that article. After an article is open, use swipe left and right gestures to navigate between pages just as you do when reading a book.

Tapping the screen displays the Reading Tools, which are the same as the ebook Read Tools.

Newspaper content often contains links that make navigating the content easier. For example, when reading *The New York Times*, you can move to the next or previous articles (as available) by tapping Previous Article or Next Article.

For more information on subscription content, including when your NOOK automatically deletes subscription content, **see** Chapter 17.

This chapter covered a lot of information on reading content on your NOOK. However, your NOOK is only one device of many that provides access to your My NOOK Library. You can also read content on your computer, your iPhone, and other devices as well.

CHAPTER 14

Lending and Borrowing Books on Your NOOK Using LendMe

To keep readers from sharing ebooks with all their friends, publishers usually protect ebooks with digital rights management (DRM), which ties an ebook to an individual, and unless that individual can prove that he is an authorized reader, the ebook will not open.

DRM is one of the reasons some people don't like ebooks. After all, when readers find a good read, they like to pass it on to friends and family. The number of people with whom you can share a physical book is fairly limited, but because ebooks are digital copies of a book, they can literally be shared with millions of people quite easily via email, Facebook, and any number of other methods.

One of the unique features that B&N added to your NOOK is the ability to lend some ebooks to other readers using the LendMe feature. Although there are some serious restrictions when lending and borrowing books, the LendMe feature is a step in the right direction.

Lending Books with LendMe

To lend a book to someone, the book must support LendMe. Not all books do. If a book does support lending, you see the LendMe logo on the book's page on bn.com, as shown in Figure 14.1. You also see the LendMe banner on the book's cover in the Library on your NOOK and in the NOOK App.

LendMe™   This NOOKbook is Lendable How it works

FIGURE 14.1   The LendMe logo appears on a book's page at bn.com if the book is lendable.

TIP: To see just a list of LendMe books, go to the Library and choose LendMe from the Type drop-down. You are presented with only LendMe NOOK Books.

To lend a book to someone using LendMe, follow these steps:

1. Browse to the book on your NOOK, and double-tap the cover to see the Details screen.

TIP: If you view only LendMe NOOK Books in the Library, you can tap the cover to immediately open the LendMe screen.

2. Tap LendMe. The LendMe screen appears.

3. Tap Contacts to select someone from your contacts, or tap Facebook to send the offer via Facebook.

4. Tap Next.

5. Tap Select a Contact to add a contact to receive this LendMe offer; select the contact and tap Done. Type a message to send with the lend invitation. (The message is optional.). The same goes for Facebook LendMe offers, but Select a Contact is instead Select Friend.

6. Tap Send or Post.

Your NOOK then displays a message that it's taking care of your LendMe request. When that message disappears, you're taken back to your Library.

What Happens If I Lend My Friend a Book She Already Owns?

If you attempt to lend a book to a friend who already owns the book you're lending, a lending error occurs. On your NOOK, you simply see a message that says, "Sorry, Your LendMe Request Was Not Possible." On the NOOK for PC app, you see an error that says, "Lending Error." Unfortunately, B&N doesn't provide any useful information about why the failure occurred, so you're left to wonder if it's because your friend already owns the book or if something else went wrong.

> If you see a lending error when attempting to lend a friend a book, check with your friend to see whether she owns the book already. If she does not yet own the book, contact B&N for information on why the LendMe attempt failed.

Choose carefully when lending a book because after you lend a book, you can never lend that particular book to anyone again. However, a book is considered to be on loan only if your friend accepts the LendMe offer. If your friend rejects the offer or if she allows the offer to expire without accepting it, you can lend the book again after it's returned to My Library.

> **I Want to Lend a Book to One of My Friends. Does My Friend Have to Own a NOOK for Me to Lend Her a Book?**
>
> No. Your friend can read an ebook you've lent to her using a NOOK App for PC, iPod Touch, iPhone, or iPad; NOOK Study; or eReader for Mac or Blackberry. However, your friend cannot read the book unless the email address you used to send the LendMe offer is associated with her B&N account.

The person to whom you've loaned the ebook has 7 days to accept the loan offer. If she doesn't accept within 7 days, the book is returned to your library. The loan offer can also be rejected, in which case the book is returned to your library immediately.

You see notifications in the status bar about your loaned ebook if your friend accepts the loan offer or rejects the loan offer and when the loaned book has been automatically returned to your library. Loan offers and notifications are visible on the status bar and on your NOOK.

While an ebook is loaned, On Loan appears next to the title in the Library and you cannot read the book. When you loan a book, you also loan your DRM rights to the book. Only one person can possess the DRM rights to a book at any one time, so you need to wait until the book is returned to your library before you can read the book again.

> **If My Friend Finishes a Loaned Book Before 14 Days Have Elapsed, Can She Return the Book to Me Immediately?**
>
> Yes. Your friend can click the Return It link that appears in the book's listing in the NOOK App. However, you cannot manually return a book using your NOOK.

There are many reports of LendMe emails not ever being received. In my use of the LendMe feature, I have experienced this on two occasions. In these situations, your friend might use the NOOK for PC app or My NOOK Library on bn.com to accept or reject the offer. In some cases, however, the offer doesn't appear in the NOOK App or My NOOK Library. B&N's answer to this problem is to wait for 7 days when the loan offer expires and then lend the book again. There isn't a way to force a re-send of the offer email, and there's no way to cancel the offer.

Borrowing Books

When a friend lends you a book, you can see the loan offer in the status bar (or in your NOOK App or on the NOOK Color and via email, and so on). You have 7 days to either accept the offer or reject it. You can accept or reject the loan offer from your NOOK.

If you accept a loan offer from your NOOK, that book is also available for the loan period in the NOOK Apps, NOOK Color, and vice versa. However, if you accept the offer from the NOOK App and then try to read the book on your NOOK, your NOOK might not realize that you've accepted the offer and might ask you to accept the offer again. When you do, the LendMe request will fail, and you'll see a message telling you that the LendMe request was not successful. When this happens, tap the Synch button from the Library, and your NOOK synchronizes with the loan offer you accepted in the NOOK App. You can then read the book you were loaned without any problems.

You can determine how much time is left on your loan period by tapping Library from the Quick Nav Bar and tapping LendMe from the Type drop-down list. The banner on the cover shows the time left. If you don't finish the book within the loan period, you can buy the book (or go into a B&N store and read in the store). When you buy a book that was lent to you, the lent copy is immediately returned to your friend.

CHAPTER 15

Using Highlights, Bookmarks, and Annotations

Take a look at one of your favorite books, and you can likely find notes in the margins and perhaps dog-eared pages. Jotting down notes about passages that impact you or marking pages you want to come back to visit later is how you make books personalized possessions. Fortunately, you don't have to forgo these things when using ebooks because your NOOK Color enables you to easily highlight passages and add bookmarks and notes to pages.

> NOTE: Your NOOK, NOOK Color, NOOK First Edition, NOOK Apps, Barnes & Noble eReader for Blackberry, and NOOK Study all support adding highlights and notes. However, notes and highlights entered in the eReader software are not shared with other devices. On the NOOK Color, NOOK, NOOK Apps, and NOOK Study, if you add a note or highlight on one device, that note or highlight is available on another device—except for the Barnes & Noble eReader app.

Using Highlights, Notes, and Bookmarks on Your NOOK

When you think of highlighting something in a book, you typically think of using a yellow highlighter marker to draw attention to portions of the text. Highlighting on your NOOK is similar to that.

A note in an ebook is simply a highlighted area with a message attached. Therefore, the steps necessary to add, view, edit, and delete notes are the same as the steps for using highlights.

Adding a Highlight or a Note

To highlight text or add a note in an ebook, follow these steps:

1. Press and hold a word. The word appears in a bubble, and that is your signal to raise your finger. The word is highlighted and the Text Selection toolbar appears.

2. If you want to highlight only that word, move to step 3. If you want to highlight a block of text, notice the highlighted word is bounded by two black bars. Press, hold, and drag one of the bars to the location you want to end the highlight.

> NOTE: The initial word highlighted must always be the first or last word in the highlight.

3. Tap Highlight to just add a highlight. Tap Note if you want to add a note. If you chose the former, the text is highlighted. If you chose the latter, the Add Note screen appears.

4. Type your note and tap Done.

5. The highlight is added, and a Note icon appears next in the margin.

Viewing, Editing, and Deleting Highlights and Notes

The simplest way to edit a note is to tap the highlighted text. A menu appears, giving you several options:

- ▶ **View Note**: Tap this to view the note. This appears only if a note is attached to that highlight. After you are in the note, you can tap Edit to edit the note.

- ▶ **Edit Note**: Tap this to edit the text of the note. This appears only if a note is attached to that highlight.

- ▶ **Add Note**: Tap this to add a note to highlighted text. An Add Note screen appears. Type in your note and tap Done. This appears only if no note is attached to that highlight.

- ▶ **Remove Note**: Tap this to remove the note. The highlight remains. This appears only if a note is attached to that highlight.

- ▶ **Remove Highlight**: Tap this to delete both the note and highlight.

> TIP: You can view the note text by tapping the Note icon on the page. From there, you can then tap Edit to edit the text of the note.

To navigate or jump to notes throughout an ebook, from the Reading Tools toolbar (tap the screen), tap Content. Then tap Notes & Highlights. You see a listing of the notes in the ebook. (Scroll if you need to see more.) You see the text that was highlighted, the page number of the note, and the date and time it was last edited. Tap the particular note you want to jump to. The contents screen disappears, and you go to the page with the highlight or note you tapped.

A couple of other notes about this screen's contents. Two other options exist: Clear All and Notes & Highlights On/Off. If you tap Clear All, you delete all notes and highlights in the ebook. If you turn Notes & Highlights to Off, you turn off the visibility of the highlights and notes. You can turn Notes & Highlights back to On to have the highlights and highlights reappear.

Using Bookmarks

Bookmarks enable you to easily return to a particular page. Unlike notes, bookmarks do not have any text associated with them. Bookmarks work in all your ebooks, magazines, and newspapers.

For ebooks, magazines, and newspapers, to add a bookmark on the page you're reading, tap the reading screen, and then tap the icon that looks like a bookmark in the top-right corner. It drops down a bit and changes to black. Tap it again to remove the bookmark. Alternatively, you can tap the upper-right corner of the screen to place a bookmark or tap the bookmark to remove it.

To return to a bookmark, from the Reading Tools toolbar, tap Content and then tap Bookmarks. A list of pages containing bookmarks appears. Tap the bookmark you want to go to; your NOOK immediately takes you to that page.

Tap Clear All to remove all bookmarks in that ebook, magazine, or newspaper.

CHAPTER 16

Using the Social Features of Your NOOK

As I'm sure you know, Facebook and Twitter are big deals these days—everyone is sharing everything. The NOOK makes this sharing even easier. You can share your reading status, share quotes, and rate and recommend books. You can share to specific contacts, on BN.com, Facebook, and Twitter. Because many of these options overlap and at the same time are scattered across the interface, this chapter focuses on Facebook sharing and the NOOK Friends app.

> NOTE: Although the locations for the sharing features are scattered, they make sense in their location. Basically, B&N provides many locations for the sharing features to make it easy to share.

> NOTE: For LendMe coverage, **see** Chapter 14, "Lending and Borrowing Books on Your NOOK Using LendMe."
>
> Using Facebook and Twitter features requires that you link your Facebook and Twitter accounts to your NOOK. **See** "Social Menu" in Chapter 2, "Customizing and Configuring Your NOOK Color," for linking your accounts.

> NOTE: The social features work only for NOOK Books, magazines, and newspapers purchased from B&N.

You can access the Facebook social features by double-tapping a cover image and tapping Share, tapping More and then tapping Share from the Reading Tools toolbar, or tapping Share from the Text Selection toolbar. Now let's deal with each of these contexts in turn.

Using Share from the Library or Reading Tools Toolbar

Double-tapping a cover either from the Library or from the Reading Tools toolbar displays the View Details Screen. Tap Share and then tap Recommend to see your recommend options: Contacts, Facebook, and Twitter. Tap Facebook and then Next to see the Facebook Recommendation screen—if you are not currently connected to a Wi-Fi hotspot, your NOOK asks you to connect to one.

To post to your Facebook wall:

1. Tap Post to My Wall.

2. Type your message that will appear. As you type, you see the number of available characters (max of 420) go down, giving you an indication of how much space you have left.

3. Tap Post. Your NOOK sends the recommendation to your wall.

If you want to post to a friend's wall, tap Post to a Friend's wall and then tap Select Friend. You can search for a name. To select a friend, tap the button on the right of the name. Tap Done. Type your message and then tap Post. Your NOOK sends the recommendation to your friend's wall.

Some other options you have are: Post Reading Status, Rate and Review, and Like on Facebook.

▶ **Post Reading Status**: This option enables you to post how far along you are in reading this NOOK Book to Facebook or Twitter. A brief headline indicating how far you are into the NOOK Book and its title is followed by the synopsis of the NOOK Book as found on BN.com.

 After tapping Share and tapping Post Reading Status, tap the check box for Facebook or Twitter (or both) and then tap Post. The update is sent.

▶ **Rate and Review**: Tapping this allows you to rate and review the book on BN.com, which appears on the B&N book's specific web page. You must provide both a rating and either a headline or review before you can post. After you tap Post, the information is sent to BN.com.

▶ **Like on Facebook**: This option enables you to post to your Facebook wall that you like this book. Tap this link and your NOOK makes the connection that you like that NOOK Book.

Using Share from the Text Selection Toolbar

Use this share function when you have a quote you want others to see. You can share on Facebook, with a contact, or on Twitter:

1. Press and hold the word you want to start the quote.

2. When the Text Selection toolbar appears, finish highlighting the quote by dragging to the end of the text you want.

3. Tap Share.

4. Tap Facebook, and then tap Next.

5. Tap either Post to My Wall or Post to a Friend's Wall.

   For Post to My Wall, type a message and tap Post.

   For Post to a Friend's Wall, tap Select Friend. Select your friend and tap Done. Type your message. Tap Post.

The appropriate wall or walls are updated.

What About Twitter and Contacts?

NOOK's support for Twitter and Contacts functions identically to Facebook, except that you share with specific contacts via email or your Twitter feed. Twitter has a more limited character count, however.

Using NOOK Friends

NOOK Friends is, to quote B&N, "the place for people who love to share their love for reading!" Here, you can connect with friends to lend and borrow books, see what your friends have been doing, and other things.

You access NOOK Friends by double-tapping a cover in the library and tapping Share. Then tap View Friends' Activity. You are already set up with an account. NOOK Friends shows what your friends have been reading, what they are recommending, how far along they are in a book, and more. If you tap Details, you are shown the details for that title.

Adding Friends

If you want to add a friend or accept a request, tap Settings from the Quick Nav Bar, tap Social, and tap Manage My NOOK Friends. A screen appears with your existing friends. If you tap one of your friend's name, you see a screen that show which of their books are available to borrow. Tap Requests when someone requests to be your NOOK Friend, which you can accept or decline. Tap Sent to see which NOOK Friends requests you have sent.

To send a request to become a NOOK Friend, tap the plus button. The Add NOOK Friends screen appears.

All Contacts displays to see all of your contacts. Tap Invite to invite that contact, and they are sent an email as well as see the request on their NOOK. Tap Suggested to see a filtered list of your contact that B&N knows already has a B&N account. You can also add a new contact by tapping Add New. Enter their first and last names and the email address. Leave the Invite as NOOK Friend check box marked to send that contact a request to become a NOOK Friend. Tap Save to send the request and save the contact.

Controlling What LendME Books Your NOOK Friends Can See

Ever had a friend see a book of yours and request to borrow it and you felt that you had to loan it even though it was the next book you wanted to read? Well, on your NOOK, you can hide any of your NOOK Books that have LendMe capability so that your friends cannot see it to request to borrow it.

First, make sure you have an active Wi-Fi connection. Then from the Quick Nav Bar, tap Settings, and then tap Social. Tap Manage Visibility of My LendMe Books. On the screen that appears, you see a list of any LendMe books you own that your friends could request. To turn off specific book from being seen, scroll to that title, and tap Show so that the slider changes to Hide. Tap Hide to switch it back to Show.

If you don't want to show any of your LendMe books to your friends, tap the check box with the long label Show All My Lendable Books to My NOOK Friends so that the checkmark is removed.

CHAPTER 17

Shopping and Visiting B&N on Your NOOK

One of the greatest features of your NOOK is the capability to sample and buy content from B&N directly from the device. As long as you have a Wi-Fi connection, you can get new content for your NOOK no matter where you are. However, you can also use the B&N website to sample and purchase content for your NOOK.

> NOTE: Only customers with billing addresses in the Unites States, Canada, or a U.S. territory can order content from the B&N NOOK Store. Citizens of U.S. territories cannot preorder items.

Shopping on Your NOOK

To shop on your NOOK, from the Quick Nav Bar, tap the Shop button. Your NOOK establishes a network connection using Wi-Fi (assuming it has one) and displays the NOOK Store Home screen, what B&N calls the *shopfront*.

Browsing the NOOK Store

The shopfront is divided up a lot like the Home screen. You have Browse Shop, Popular Lists, and Picks. To start browsing, tap Browse. The Browse Shop and Popular Lists are existing options within the overall Browse list, so tap one of those if you want to jump right to browsing books or new releases. In addition to collections such as NOOK Books, Magazines, and Newspapers, you also see special collections such as NOOK Books Under $5 and LendMe NOOK Books.

At the bottom of the shopfront is a section displaying picks (B&N Recommends, Jules' Picks, and so on). These are often based on your past purchase or browsing history. Also some deals are tossed in there as well.

Searching for Content

If you want to find a particular item in the NOOK Store, tap Search and enter your search terms. Your NOOK displays the results of your search after several seconds. The results show all the items in which your search terms appear in one or more of the following:

- Title

- Author

- Publisher

- Subject

- Contributors

When your search results appear, you can view the results by covers in Grid view or by list view. Additionally, you can sort by choosing Top Matches, Best Selling, Title, Price, or Release Date by tapping the drop-down list.

Sampling and Buying Content

After you locate and select an item you're interested in, double-tap the cover to see an overview page that describes the item and shows the rating of the item from other B&N readers. In addition, you see the following options:

- **Overview**: Displays the default view when you select an item. You can tap the stars to give the NOOK Book a rating, tap Share to access the social options, or tap My Wishlist to add this title to your wishlist.

> NOTE: This wishlist is *not* the same wishlist as on BN.com or on your NOOK Color. Treat all three wishlists as separate lists. Perhaps some day, B&N will have one synchronized wishlist.

- **Reviews**: Displays editorial and customer reviews for the item. Editorial reviews often show details from the publisher along with critic reviews of the item. It can span multiple pages. Customer reviews are comments from other B&N customers.

- **Related Titles**: Displays either more titles by this author or more titles that other people purchased along with the book you are looking at. Tap the cover to see information about that title.

If you like what you see, you can download a sample to your NOOK by tapping Free Sample. (Sampling is only valid with NOOK Books.) Samples typically consist of the first chapter of an ebook. However, it's up to the publisher to decide what to provide as a sample. In some cases, samples might contain just a few pages. In other cases, samples consist primarily of front matter, such as the title page, table of contents, dedication, and so on. One sample I downloaded contained nine pages of front matter and two pages of actual manuscript—hardly enough to actually get a feel for the book.

> NOTE: Samples never expire. You can keep a sample for as long as you want.

If you decide to buy a book after reading the sample, tap Buy; the book is then added to your library. Because samples and full ebooks are completely separate products, a purchased book does not open at the point where the sample ended. You need to manually navigate to the point where you stopped reading the sample.

> NOTE: If a B&N gift card is associated with your account, the cost for items purchased from the B&N NOOK Store are applied against that gift card. If there is not enough credit left on the card, B&N charges the remaining balance to your credit card on file.

If you'd like to remove a sample from your NOOK, you have to visit My NOOK Library at bn.com from your computer or archive the sample in the Library. If you delete a sample unintentionally, you can download it again.

For more information on using My NOOK Library, **see** Chapter 20, "Using My NOOK Library."

Is It Possible to Accidentally Purchase a Book I Previously Purchased from B&N's NOOK Store?

Your NOOK does not even present the option to purchase a book you already own. If you select a book in the NOOK Store that you already own, you are shown an option to download or read the book, depending upon whether the book is already on your NOOK. However, you will not be shown an option to buy the book.

Some classic titles are released by multiple publishers. Two books of the same title from two different publishers are not considered the same title, so in these cases, you can purchase the same book twice.

Subscription content also enables you to sample prior to purchasing, but it works a bit differently than it does with ebooks. When you subscribe to a newspaper or magazine, you receive a 14-day free trial. If you cancel your subscription within that 14-day period, you will not be charged. If you cancel after the 14-day trial period, you will be refunded a prorated amount based on when you cancel.

You can use a trial subscription only once for any particular item. For example, if you subscribe to *The Wall Street Journal* and cancel your subscription within the 14-day trial period, you will be charged beginning immediately if you were to subscribe to *The Wall Street Journal* again because you have already taken advantage of a trial subscription.

> NOTE: Subscriptions can be canceled only using My NOOK Library at bn.com. You cannot cancel a subscription using your NOOK.

Your NOOK automatically downloads subscription content when it's available. In addition to seeing the new content in the Library, you'll also receive notifications in The Daily for any new subscription content your NOOK downloads.

Using Your NOOK in a B&N Store

As mentioned earlier, B&N stores have a Wi-Fi hotspot, so your NOOK can access free Wi-Fi while in the store. B&N uses this hotspot to offer you special promotions called More in Store while in the store. Your NOOK can automatically connect to a B&N hotspot when in the store, but you do need to ensure that Wi-Fi is turned on. (It's on by default.)

After your NOOK connects to the B&N hotspot, tap Shop (which now displays an In-Store banner) from the Quick Nav Bar. One of the banners in the store has links for Read in Store, More in Store, Browse Read in Store Books, and Read Free Content.

Tap Read in Store to see the available Read in Store books (with an In Store banner). To read in store, tap the cover, and tap Read In Store. The book downloads. Tap Read. You can read it in store for one hour a day.

More in Store contains free content. If you tap More in Store, you are shown a list of the available content. Tap the cover and tap Free. Tap Confirm. The item downloads. Tap Read to read it.

The typical More in Store offerings consist of several articles B&N feels might be interesting. You are likely to find some interesting and others that don't interest you at all. If you'd like to get a sneak preview of what's available before you drive down to your local B&N, you can browse to http://www.barnesandnoble.com/NOOK/moreinstore/, which shows the current list of free content you can download at B&N.

NOTE: You need to connect to the B&N hotspot to download and read the More in Store offerings.

When you connect to a B&N hotspot in a B&N store, you can read nearly any ebook in the B&N store for up to 1 hour. There's no doubt that B&N has a unique opportunity because of its brick-and-mortar presence. No other ebook reader has the capability of being paired with a retail outlet, certainly one of the more unique capabilities of the NOOK, and NOOK owners should be excited about what More in Store might offer in the future.

CHAPTER 18

Reading Beyond Your NOOK

If you don't have your NOOK handy, you can read items from your ebook library using the B&N NOOK Apps. B&N provides a version of the NOOK application for your PC, Mac, iPhone, iPad, iPod Touch, and Android device—even a NOOK Kids for iPad app.

NOTE: Technically, no Blackberry version of the NOOK App exists. The B&N eReader app, however, exists for the Blackberry. This is basically an older version of the NOOK App with significantly fewer features.

The experience the NOOK App provides varies depending on which device you use. On a PC, the experience similar to reading on your NOOK Color. On other devices, the experience is a bit more scaled-down.

You can download the NOOK App for your PC or another device by going to http://www.barnesandnoble.com/u/free-NOOK-apps/379002321/, clicking the appropriate NOOK App device link, and clicking the download link. (For the iPad, iPhone, or iPod Touch, you can search for Barnes & Noble NOOK in the App Store or in the iTunes Store.)

TIP: If you use a Blackberry or Android phone, B&N requires that you download the NOOK App from your device. For the Blackberry, you can do that by browsing to bn.com on your device and clicking the link to download the eReader app. For the Android version, search for NOOK in the Android Marketplace or scan the QR code on the Barnes & Noble Android NOOK App download web page.

Using the NOOK for PC App

When you launch NOOK App on your PC, you'll be asked to sign in to your B&N account. Enter your username and password, and click Sign In if you already have an account on bn.com. If you don't have an account, you can click Create an Account to create one.

> NOTE: The Mac version of the NOOK App is essentially the same as the PC version.

Browsing Your B&N Online Library with the NOOK for PC App

After you sign in to your account the NOOK for PC app checks in with My NOOK Library and synchronizes samples, last pages read, etc. You then see a series of buttons along the left side that mirror the buttons you see on your NOOK's touchscreen when at the Home screen (see Figure 18.1). The only difference you notice is that the order of the Shop and Reading Now buttons is reversed on NOOK for PC app versus your NOOK.

FIGURE 18.1   The menu buttons in the NOOK for PC app mirror several of those on your NOOK.

By default, NOOK for PC app displays ebooks and subscription content. However, you can filter the view to show only ebooks, magazines, newspapers, and manually added content (what B&N calls "my stuff") by clicking the appropriate option in the My Library menu.

Along the top of the NOOK for PC app are buttons to manually refresh your library, control the views of your library, sort your library, and search your library, as shown in Figure 18.2.

FIGURE 18.2   Function buttons at the top of NOOK for PC app enable you to control how you view your library.

Clicking the Sync button synchronizes your B&N NOOK Library with the NOOK for PC app. Use this to synchronize your notes and page location.

> NOTE: When the original NOOK and NOOK Apps were created, B&N had not yet created the mechanism to synchronize between devices. With the November NOOK software update and built into the NOOK Color and NOOK Apps, synchronization between these devices is now possible. No longer do you need to worry about finding your page or keeping notes across devices.

The View button (by default an image of six little boxes) controls how your ebook library appears in the NOOK for PC app. By default, the NOOK for PC app shows your library in list view. In this view, a small image of the cover of each item displays along with items such as the author, the last read date, and so on. You can switch to a grid or bookshelf view that shows only large images of each item's cover by clicking View button, as shown in Figure 18.2. When you do, the View button changes to show three parallel lines.

When you select to show your items in list view, the Cover Size button enables you to control the size of the cover image that displays. (The button shows a small rectangle.) The smallest size is slightly smaller than the size displayed when in grid view, and the largest size is approximately twice the size of the covers shown in grid view.

> NOTE: Most covers provided with ebooks and other content look terrible when you select the largest available size in list view because they're not intended for display at such a large size.

You can sort your online library in the NOOK for PC app by clicking the Sort button, which defaults to Recent, but changes to Title and Author as you continue to click it.

After you've owned your NOOK for a while, you're likely to accumulate a large digital library of content. The NOOK for PC app enables you to easily find content as your NOOK library grows; you can search your library for content. When you click inside the Search Library box, you're given a choice to search for a title, an author, a publisher, or all three, as shown in Figure 18.3. Select an option, enter your search text, and either click the magnifying glass or press Enter to search your library.

FIGURE 18.3   Searching your library using the NOOK for PC app.

TIP: Searches are filtered based on how your library is filtered. For example, if you've selected eMagazines from the My Library menu, searches show only magazines that match your search terms.

If you want to view all the items in your NOOK library instead of just those that match your search terms, click the X inside the Search Library box. Doing so clears your search term and shows all the items in your online library.

Viewing the Daily in the NOOK for PC App

Clicking the Daily menu button displays the Daily. Assuming you are connected to the Internet, it updates with the latest articles. Click Read Now to read the particular article, which appears in a small box. Clicking Close hides the article from view.

Shopping for ebooks in the NOOK for PC App

Clicking the Shop button opens up your web browser at BN.com. For more information about shopping for ebooks, **see** "Shopping on Your Computer" in Chapter 9, "Shopping and Visiting B&N on Your NOOK Color."

Reading Items in the NOOK for PC App

When you hover your mouse pointer over an item in My Library, the NOOK for PC app displays several options (see Figure 18.4):

▶ **Read Now**: Opens the item in the NOOK for PC app. If the item hasn't been downloaded to your computer, the NOOK for PC app downloads it first and then opens it.

▶ **LendMe**: Displayed only for items you can lend to friends. When clicked, it opens a dialog box for entering the email address of a friend to whom you'd like to lend the item. **See** Chapter 4, "Lending and Borrowing Books with LendMe on Your NOOK Color," for more details about the LendMe feature.

▶ **Download**: Displayed when the item hasn't been downloaded to your computer. When clicked, the item is downloaded to your local computer and Download changes to Remove Local Copy.

▶ **Remove Local Copy**: Displayed when the item has been downloaded to your local computer. When clicked, the item is removed from your local computer. If you want to read it at a later time, you need to download it again.

▶ **Move to Archive**: Moves the item to your archive. Archived items appear in the Archive category in My Library.

▶ **Unarchive**: Displayed only for archived items. When clicked, the item is moved from the archive to your main digital library.

▶ **Details**: Displays the details for the item. Details typically consist of a larger image of the cover and a brief synopsis of the item.

FIGURE 18.4 Available options for when you hover over a cover.

> TIP: Archiving or unarchiving an item in the NOOK for PC app on your PC also archives or unarchives the item on your NOOK, NOOK Color, and other apps (except the B&N Blackberry and Mac eReader apps).

While you're reading content, the NOOK for PC app displays the Reading Now menu. Using the Reading Now menu, you can easily navigate to the last page read, access the table of contents, and access bookmarks, annotations, and highlights for the item you're reading.

> NOTE: Neither annotations nor highlights are available for subscription content.

For more information on using bookmarks, highlighting, and annotations, **see** Chapter 5, "Using Highlights, Bookmarks, and Annotations."

Using Highlights, Notes, and Bookmarks in the NOOK for PC App

You can also use highlights in the NOOK for PC app. However, you cannot add highlights or notes to subscription content.

Adding Highlights and Notes

To add a highlight to an ebook in the NOOK for PC app, click your mouse on the starting point where you want your highlight. While holding the mouse button, drag your mouse to the ending point for the highlight. When you do this, the NOOK for PC app highlights the text and displays a pop-up menu (see Figure 18.5). To make the highlighted text an actual highlight, click Highlight Selection.

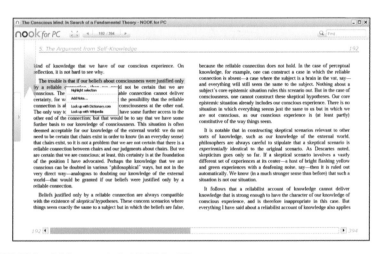

FIGURE 18.5   Adding a note in NOOK for PC app.

If you want to add a note, click Add Note from the pop-up menu. Type your note, and then click OK. If you want to add a note to text that is already defined as a highlight, highlight a portion of that text again. The pop-up menu offers a couple of extra options (see Figure 18.6). Click Add Note to add a new note to the existing highlight. Add the text for your note, and then click OK.

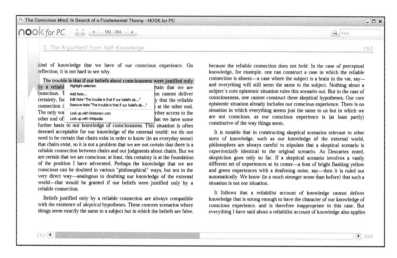

FIGURE 18.6   Editing an existing note or highlight.

Viewing Highlights and Notes

To view highlights, click Highlights under the Reading Now menu. Highlights that
don't have notes associated with them can be found by clicking Highlights. If a note
is associated with the highlight, click Annotations in the Reading Now menu to see
the note. You can quickly jump to any note or highlight by clicking the specific note
or highlight (see Figure 18.7).

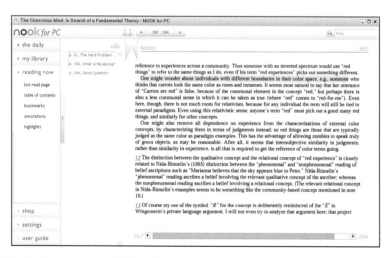

FIGURE 18.7   Jump to any highlight in a book.

> **Can I Change the Green Color the NOOK or PC App Uses for Highlights?**
> You can't change the color of highlights on the PC.

Editing and Deleting Highlights and Notes

To edit a note associated with a highlight, highlight a portion of that text that comprises the note and click Edit Note. Enter the new text for the note, and click OK. To delete the note, select Remove Note; then click Yes when asked to confirm that you want to delete the note. Follow the same steps to remove a highlight that doesn't have a note associated with it.

Using Bookmarks

To add a bookmark to a page in the NOOK for PC app, click the ribbon with pointed ends in the corner of the page. When you do, the ribbon drops down onto the page and your bookmark appears in the bookmark pane when you select Bookmarks from the Reading Now menu. To remove the bookmark, click the ribbon again.

You can easily navigate to a particular bookmark by clicking the bookmark in the bookmark pane (see Figure 18.8).

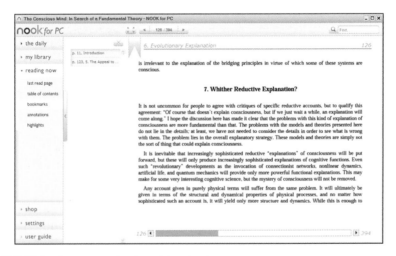

FIGURE 18.8   Jump to any bookmark in a book.

Importing Books into the NOOK for PC App

All books in your B&N online library are automatically added to the NOOK for PC app. If you want to read a book you purchased from another source, you can add it to the NOOK for PC app by clicking the My Library, clicking My Stuff menu, and then clicking the Add New Item button (see Figure 18.9).

FIGURE 18.9   Click this button to add non-B&N ebooks and content.

> NOTE: You can only import eReader format (PDB files) and EPUB format ebooks along with PDFs into the NOOK for PC app.

If the book you are importing contains DRM, you will be asked for your name and credit card information when you attempt to read the book in the NOOK for PC app. You need to supply this information only the first time you read the book.

> **Can I Read Books in Formats Other Than eReader and EPUB in the NOOK for PC App?**
>
> Kind of. To read a book in the NOOK for PC app, you must first convert the book to either eReader format or EPUB format. You can use Calibre to convert books into a format that is compatible with the NOOK for PC app, provided the book is not protected with DRM. To learn how to use Calibre, **see** Chapter 19, "Managing Your ebooks with Calibre."

Configuring the NOOK for PC App Settings

Clicking the Settings menu lets you change the appearance of content in the NOOK for PC app and change your account settings.

To change the appearance of content, click Settings and then click Reading Preferences. From this screen, you can change the font size and margin spacing used in the NOOK for PC app. Clicking the font size adjusts the sample text size to give you an idea of how it will appear when reading an actual ebook. The Margins option is controlled by clicking and dragging the Indicator icon or clicking anywhere along the bar. Toward the right increases the amount of white space on either side of the text. Toward the left decreases the amount.

> NOTE: Account Settings appears by default when you click Settings.

To change account settings, click Account Settings. You can sign in or sign out of your B&N account from this screen. You can also choose whether recent purchases are downloaded automatically. The other option you have is Autohide Navigation When Opening Reading Now. By default, this is selected, and what it means is that when you are reading an ebook, the Daily, My Library, and such, options on the left disappear. (You can get it back by clicking the left-facing arrow bar.) Otherwise, the menu is always available.

Using NOOK Apps on Your iPhone, iPod Touch, or Android Phone

The NOOK for PC application is a straightforward program. It's similar to your NOOK, and is intuitive and easy to use. The NOOK for iPhone, iPad, iPod Touch, and Android (referred to as simply the NOOK App from now on) are different from the NOOK for PC app because of the devices, but each of them still offers an easy-to-use interface.

> NOTE: As of this writing, B&N has disabled reading subscription content on the NOOK App. If you want to read content other than ebooks, you need to use either NOOK for PC app, NOOK Study app, or your NOOK.

> NOTE: The focus of this section is on the iPhone app though the iPod Touch app is identical. The Android app is essentially identical in features and general interactivity, as well, though with the quirks of the Android phone navigation vis-à-vis the quirks of the iPhone navigation.

The NOOK App launches and syncs with your NOOK library. You have quite a few options on this small screen (see Figure 18.10):

- **Shop for eBooks**: Tapping this launches the Safari web browser and opens the NOOK Store.

- **Sync**: Tapping this synchronizes page location, notes, and so on with your NOOK Library.

▶ **View**: Tapping this switches between a list and grid view. (The default is grid view.) If you change to list view, the Shop for eBooks becomes a link at the top.

▶ **Sort**: Tapping these options sorts your list by the designated category.

▶ **Type**: Tapping this lets you see either your ebooks or archived ebooks. By default, your ebooks are sorted by most recent.

▶ **Search Library**: Tapping this allows you to search your library for a specific book.

FIGURE 18.10   Though small, the NOOK App interface has a lot of options.

Browsing My NOOK Library

Browsing your library is easy; just swipe up and down with your finger to scroll.

CAUTION: Don't be surprised if while you scroll through your library, you accidentally tap the Download icon and download the book to your device.

To read an ebook, you first need to download it to your device. You can easily tell whether a book has been downloaded. If a Download button appears, you have not downloaded it to your device. Just tap the button to do so. After the ebook has been downloaded to your device, it opens so that you can begin reading.

Reading Books in the NOOK App

To read an ebook in the NOOK App, just tap the cover image to open it in reading mode. When there, to move to the next page, swipe your finger from right to left. To move to the previous page, swipe your finger from left to right. The reading screen, however, offers more options than just reading (see Figure 18.11).

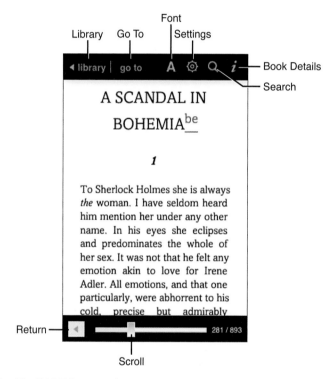

FIGURE 18.11 The NOOK App reading interface.

If you do not see the surrounding bars in the reading screen, just tap the page, and they will appear. Before discussing some of these options, take a quick tour:

▶ **Library**: Tapping this returns you to your NOOK library.

▶ **Go To**: Tapping this opens the table of contents with links to see your notes and annotations and bookmarks. You can scroll through any of these items and click the appropriate link to go quickly to that spot in the ebook.

▶ **Return**: This icon appears when you have tapped a footnote link (the blue link in Figure 18.11), going to the footnote. Tapping the Return button takes you back to the page you were originally on.

▶ **Book Details**: Tapping this brings up a page with many details related to the book.

▶ **Search**: Tapping this lets you search for specific text in this ebook.

▶ **Settings**: Tapping this lets you adjust the margin width and brightness.

▶ **Font**: Tapping this allows you to adjust the specific font, justification, colors, and font size.

Two of these screens deserve more attention: Book Details and Font. Now take a closer look at these.

Using the Book Details Screen

After tapping Book Details, you see a screen like Figure 18.12.

FIGURE 18.12   The NOOK App's Book Details screen.

As you can see, you have several options here. Tapping the X returns you to the reading screen. You can rate the ebook by tapping a star. (Tap the third star, and the first three are marked.)

> NOTE: If you give a star rating to an ebook, you cannot remove the star rating. You can only adjust it up or down.

In Figure 18.8, if you tap the right-pointing arrow next to the *Two Years Before the Mast* text, you are taken to a book synopsis. Clicking the X there returns you to the Book Details screen.

Tapping Table of Contents, Bookmarks, or Notes/Highlights quickly returns you to the reading screen and opens up the Go To page at the corresponding list of Contents, Notes, and so on. Clicking the X there returns you to the reading screen.

B&N has the unique LendMe feature for many NOOK Books. Whether you can lend NOOK Books is up to the publisher. To use this feature, just tap the LendMe icon. This takes you to another screen where you can type in the email address of the person to whom you want to lend the NOOK Book. (You can also tap the blue plus sign and select an email from your contacts.)

You can also type a message to the person. Click Send to send the offer to the person. After you've done this, you will notice in your library that the sash that once read Lendable now reads Lent. You can no longer read this book (until either the recipient turns down the offer, returns the ebook to you, or the lending time runs out).

You can also archive this book by pressing the Move to Archive icon. The Remove from Device option does just that. You can always download it again to your NOOK App by tapping Download.

Finally, you can click Shop for More by This Author to open a Safari browser window displaying other NOOK Books available from that author.

Adjusting Fonts

After tapping Fonts, you see a screen like Figure 18.13.

Again, a small screen that provides many options. The general purpose of this screen is to provide settings related to the reading experience in the NOOK App. Clicking the X closes this screen, returns you to the reading screen, and makes any changes that you have indicated.

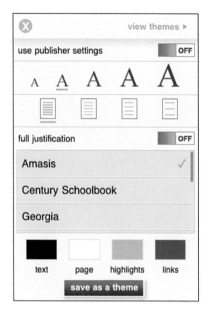

FIGURE 18.13 The NOOK App's Fonts screen.

We will come back to View Themes. You can choose Use Publisher Settings. In an ebook, the publisher often provides a series of defaults (font size, type of font, and so on). Changing this option to On sets the settings to those publisher default settings. You can change it to Off at any time you want.

Clicking the A icon adjusts the font size. The current font size has an underline beneath it.

The set of icons beneath the font size determine line spacing. Think of this like single space, double space, and so on. The current setting has a line beneath that icon.

The Full Justification setting is either On or Off (and is Off by default). I have yet to see any difference in the reading screen with this option On or Off.

Depending on what the publisher of this ebook allows, you can adjust the font. You can scroll through the available list. (A check mark appears to the right of the currently selected one.) You have options between serif and sans serif fonts. Serif is a technical term that refers to the "hanging structure" on a letter. In Figure 18.13, if you look at the A icons, notice the little base at the bottom of each leg of the A? That's a serif. Sans (French for "without") serif fonts lack these structures. In general, most people find reading serif fonts easier on the eyes. Unfortunately, the fonts in the Fonts screen don't give you a preview, so you may need to experiment a bit to find the one you like best.

> NOTE: Of the available font options Amasis, Century Schoolbook, Georgia, Joanna, and Times New Roman are serif fonts. Ascender Sans, Gill Sans, and Trebuchet MS are sans serif fonts.

The bottom part of this screen gives you options for color related to the text, highlights, page, and links. Tap it and you end up in the reading screen color options screen. Figure 18.14 shows the basic screen for adjusting the color for all four of these items.

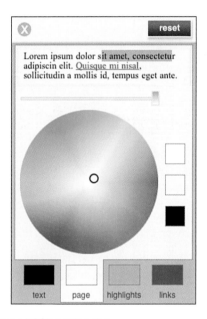

FIGURE 18.14 Altering the NOOK app's color.

Basically, you have a lot of colors to choose from. Your first task is to select the particular part of the reading screen you want to change the color on: Text, Page, Highlights, or Links. The top part of the screen with the nonsense Latin "Lorem ipsum dolor..." reflects the alterations you make here. Thus, change the text to red, and the Lorem ipsum text changes to red.

The three squares next to the color wheel offer three quick ways of applying color. The black square adjusts whatever color you are changing to black. In other words, if you tap Links and then tap the black square next to the color wheel, the links appear in black. (In the Lorem ipsum text, the Quisque mi nisal link text changes from the default blue color to black.) The white square on top changes the color wheel from solid black to what you see in Figure 18.14. Tap an area of the wheel to choose that color for the item.

So what's the middle tan square for? Tap it and it changes the selected item to a neutral color (works great for the page background). Tap Reset or the X icon to save your changes.

The world of colors for your ebook reading brings us to themes. On the Fonts screen there are two theme-related buttons: View Themes and Save as a Theme. Tap Save as a Theme and a screen appears prompting you to provide a name for the theme. (You can see the default themes: The Printed Page, Night Light, and so on.) Assuming you like the color set you have, give them a name, tap Done, and tap Save Theme. If you have a theme or you want to use one of the default themes, tap View Themes and tap the theme you want. A check mark appears next to the selected them. Tap the X icon to apply the theme. If you tap Edit, you can change the name of the themes (including the default ones).

Deleting a theme is as easy as tapping View Themes, tapping Edit, tapping the circle next to the theme you want to delete, and tapping Delete Selection.

Adding Notes and Highlights in the NOOK App

Adding Notes, Highlights, and Bookmarks in the NOOK App is as easy as using your finger to select the part of the ebook to which you want to add a note or highlight. Here's how you do it:

1. Using your finger, select the text you want to add a Note or Highlight to. The text will be highlighted according to the Font settings' Highlight color. As soon as you lift your finger from the selection, the Notes & Highlights screen opens (see Figure 18.15).

2. Tap Highlight to add the highlight and nothing else.

   Tap Add Note to go to the Add Notes screen, where you can type in a note and tap Save.

If you select a single word, the Search Dictionary is an available option. Tapping it brings up a dictionary entry for the word. Tapping See More Definitions Online opens a Safari browser at Dictionary.com. Tapping the X icon takes you back to the reading screen.

Tapping Google or Wikipedia opens a Safari browser with the text you selected entered as the search criteria.

3. The note and highlights are available for easy access using the Go To menu from the reading screen.

FIGURE 18.15   The Note & Highlights screen.

Although the NOOK App saves your location in reading, you may still want to add a bookmark. In the reading screen, but without the options bars, in the bottom-right corner, you see a plus sign (see Figure 18.16). Tap it to set a bookmark. Tap it again to remove the bookmark.

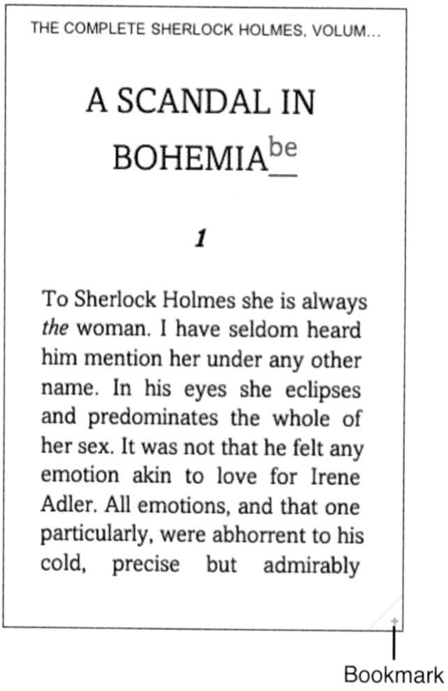

THE COMPLETE SHERLOCK HOLMES, VOLUM...

A SCANDAL IN
BOHEMIA^{be}

1

To Sherlock Holmes she is always *the* woman. I have seldom heard him mention her under any other name. In his eyes she eclipses and predominates the whole of her sex. It was not that he felt any emotion akin to love for Irene Adler. All emotions, and that one particularly, were abhorrent to his cold, precise but admirably

Bookmark

FIGURE 18.16   Tap the plus sign to set a bookmark.

Using the NOOK for iPad App

The NOOK for iPad app is a larger version of the NOOK for iPhone app adapted to the larger screen size of the iPad.

> NOTE: As of this writing, you can read newspaper and some magazines from B&N has on the NOOK for iPad app. Make sure to check the available apps and devices you can read a particular magazine on at BN.com prior to purchasing. You will see what apps and devices you can read that magazine on at the magazine's product page. However, even if you cannot read a magazine on the NOOK for iPad app, its cover will still appear in that library.

The NOOK App launches and syncs with your NOOK library. This default Home screen has many similarities to the NOOK for iPhone app, though adjusted for the more spacious real estate of the iPad (see Figure 18.17).

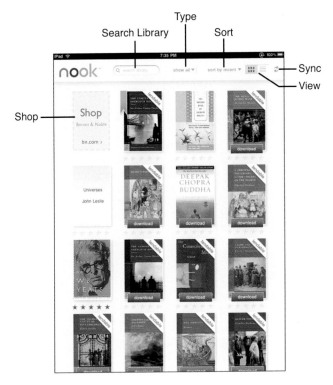

FIGURE 18.17   The NOOK App for iPad home page.

Now take a look at the options available on this screen:

▶ **Shop for eBooks**: Tapping this launches the Safari web browser and opens the B&N NOOK Store.

▶ **Sync**: Tapping this synchronizes page location, notes, and so on with your NOOK Library.

▶ **View**: Tapping one of the two options organizes this Home screen. The default is the grid view. You can switch to an individual book view by tapping the right button (the one with four lines)—see Figure 18.18. Switch back to grid view by tapping the left button (the one with six boxes). The individual book view offers a scrolling list of your library and detailed information about the current book, which is covered here in a bit.

▶ **Sort**: Tapping these options sorts your list by the designated category.

▶ **Type**: Tapping this lets you see either your ebooks or archived ebooks. By default, your ebooks are sorted by most recent.

▶ **Search Library**: Tapping this allows you to search your library for a specific book.

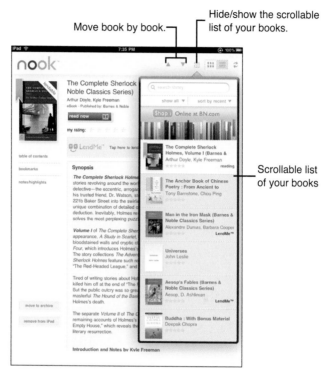

FIGURE 18.18   Book-by-book view in the NOOK for iPad app.

Browsing My NOOK Library

Browsing your library is easy; just swipe up and down with your finger to scroll.

To read an ebook, you first need to download it to your device. You can easily tell whether a book has been downloaded. If a Download button appears, you have not downloaded it. Just tap the button to do so. The ebook will be downloaded to your device. After the ebook has been downloaded, it will open to begin reading.

Reading Books in the NOOK for iPad App

To read an ebook in the NOOK App, just tap the cover image to open it in reading mode. When there, to move to the next page, swipe your finger from right to left.

To move to the previous page, swipe your finger from left to right. The reading screen, however, offers more options than just reading (see Figure 18.19).

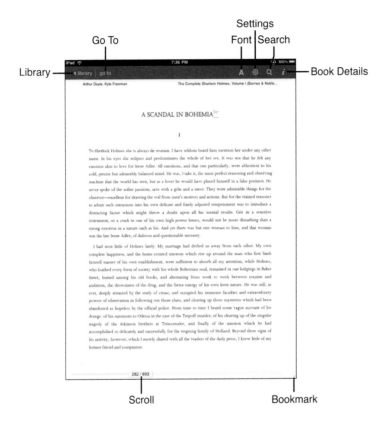

FIGURE 18.19   The NOOK for iPad app reading interface.

If you do not see the surrounding bars in the reading screen, just tap the page and they will appear. Before exploring some of these options, take a quick tour:

- ▶ **Library**: Tapping this returns you to your NOOK library.

- ▶ **Go To**: Tapping this opens the table of contents with links to see your notes and annotations and bookmarks. You can scroll through any of these items and click the appropriate link to go quickly to that spot in the ebook.

- ▶ **Bookmark**: Tapping this adds a bookmark to this page.

- ▶ **Book Details**: Tapping this brings up a page with many details related to the book.

▶ **Search**: Tapping this lets you search for specific text in this ebook.

▶ **Settings**: Tapping this lets you adjust the margin width and brightness.

▶ **Font**: Tapping this allows you to adjust the specific font, justification, colors, and font size.

Two of these screens deserve more attention: Book Details and Font. Now take a closer look at these.

Using the Book Details Screen

After tapping Book Details, you see a screen like Figure 18.20.

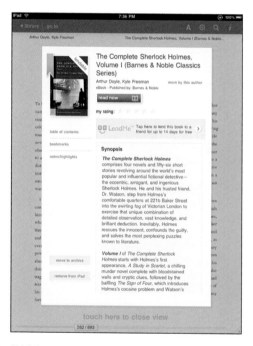

FIGURE 18.20   The NOOK App's Book Details screen.

In the NOOK for iPad app, two versions of this screen exist. Figure 18.20 shows the screen as it appears by tapping the Book Details button from within the reading screen. If you are in individual book view at the Home screen, you see a slightly larger version of this same page. Also, if you press and hold a cover image in grid view, a similar Book Details screen appears (refer to Figure 18.20). All the functionality between the different versions of the Book Details screen is the same.

As you can see, you have several options here. Tapping an area outside of the Book Details screen returns you to the reading screen. You can rate the ebook by tapping a star. (Tap the third star, and the first three are marked.)

NOTE: If you give a star rating to an ebook, you cannot remove the star rating. You can only adjust it up or down.

Tapping Table of Contents, Bookmarks, or Notes/Highlights quickly returns you to the reading screen and opens the Go To page at the corresponding list of Contents, Notes, and so on. Tapping outside the Table of Contents, Bookmarks, or Notes/Highlights part of the screen, returns you to the reading screen.

B&N has the unique LendMe feature for many NOOK Books. Whether you can lend NOOK Books is up to the publisher. To use this feature, just tap the LendMe icon. This takes you to another screen where you can type in the email address of the person you want to lend the NOOK Book to. (You can also tap the blue plus sign and select an email from your contacts.)

You can also type a message to the person. Tap Send to send the offer to the person. After you do this, you can notice in your library that the sash that once read Lendable now reads Lent. You can no longer read this book (until either the recipient turns down the offer, returns the ebook to you, or the lending time runs out).

You can also archive this book by pressing the Move to Archive icon. The Remove from iPad option does just that. You can always download it again to your NOOK for iPad app by tapping Download.

Finally, you can click the More by This Author to open a Safari browser window displaying other NOOK Books available from that author.

Adjusting Fonts

After tapping Fonts, you see a screen like Figure 18.21. (The Fonts screen for newspapers and magazines has fewer options, though the ones there function the same.)

The general purpose of this screen is to provide settings related to the reading experience in the NOOK App. Tapping outside the Fonts screen closes it, returns you to the reading screen, and makes any changes that you have indicated.

Now back to View Themes. You can choose Use Publisher Settings. In an ebook, the publisher often provides a series of defaults (font size, type of font, and so on). Changing this option to On sets the settings to those publisher default settings. You can change it to Off at any time you want.

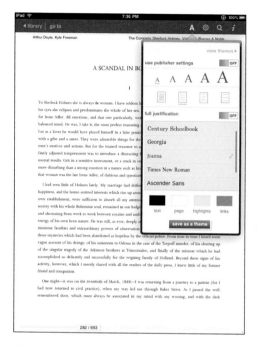

FIGURE 18.21   The NOOK for iPad app's Fonts screen.

Tapping the A icon adjusts the font size. The current font size has an underline beneath it.

The set of icons beneath the font size determines line spacing. Think of this like single space, double space, and so on. The current setting has a line beneath that icon.

The Full Justification setting is either On or Off (and is Off by default). I have yet to see any difference in the reading screen with this option On or Off.

Depending on what the publisher of this ebook allows, you can adjust the font. You can scroll through the available list. (A check mark appears to the right of the currently selected one.) You have options between serif and sans serif fonts. What is this? Serif is a technical term that refers to the "hanging structure" on a letter. In Figure 18.21, if you look at the A icons, notice the little base at the bottom of each leg of the A? That's a serif. Sans (French for "without") serif fonts lack these structures. In general, most people find reading serif fonts easier on the eyes.

NOTE: Of the available font options, Amasis, Century Schoolbook, Georgia, Joanna, and Times New Roman are serif fonts. Ascender Sans, Gill Sans, and Trebuchet MS are sans serif fonts.

The bottom part of this screen gives you options for color related to the text, highlights, page, and links. Tap it and you end up in the reading screen color options screen. Figure 18.22 shows the basic screen for adjusting the color for all four of these items.

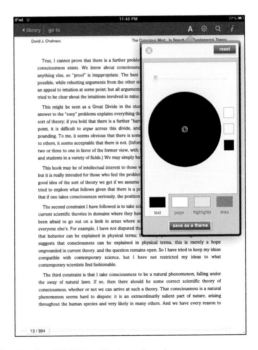

FIGURE 18.22   Altering the NOOK for iPad app's color.

Basically, you have a lot of colors to choose from. Your first task is to select the particular part of the reading screen you want to change the color on: Text, Page, Highlights, or Links.

The three squares next to the color wheel offer three quick ways to apply color. The black square adjusts whatever color you change to black. In other words, if you tap Links and then tap the black square next to the color wheel, the links appear in black. The white square on top changes the color wheel from solid black to a rainbow of colors. Tap an area of the wheel to choose that color for the item.

So what's the middle tan square for? Tap it and it changes the selected item to a neutral color (works great for the page background). Tap Reset or the X icon to save your changes.

The world of colors for your ebook reading brings us to themes. On the Fonts screen there are two theme-related buttons: View Themes and Save as a Theme. Tap Save as a Theme, and a screen appears prompting you to provide a name for the theme. (You can see the default themes: The Printed Page, Night Light, and so on.) Assuming you like the color setup you have, give them a name, tap Done, and tap Save Theme. If you have a theme or you want to use one of the default themes, tap View Themes and tap the theme you want. A check mark appears next to the selected them. Tap the X icon to apply the theme. If you tap Edit, you can change the name of the themes (including the default ones).

Deleting a theme is as easy as tapping View Themes, tapping Edit, tapping the circle next to the theme you want to delete, and tapping Delete Selection.

Adding Notes and Highlights in the NOOK for iPad App

Adding Notes, Highlights, and Bookmarks in the NOOK for iPad app is as easy as using your finger to select the part of the ebook you want to add a note or whatever to. Here's how you do it:

1. Using your finger, press and hold until you see the word your finger is on become highlighted; then select the text you want to add a Note or Highlight to. (If you just want that word, you can lift your finger.) The text will be highlighted according to the Font settings' Highlight color. As soon as you lift your finger from the selection, the Note & Highlights screen opens (see Figure 18.23).

2. Tap Highlight to add the highlight and nothing else.

   Tap Add Note to be taken to the Add Notes screen, where you can type in a note and tap Save Note.

   If you selected a single word, the Search Dictionary is an available option. Tapping it brings up a dictionary entry for the word. Tapping See More Definitions Online opens a Safari browser at Dictionary.com. Tapping outside the definition screen takes you back to the reading screen.

   Tapping Google or Wikipedia opens a Safari browser with the text you selected entered as the search criteria.

3. The note and highlights are available for easy access using the Go To menu from the reading screen.

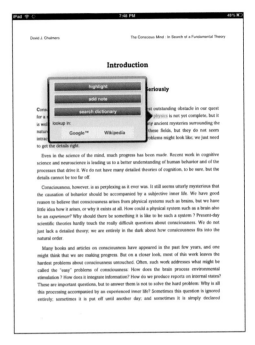

FIGURE 18.23   The Note & Highlights screen.

Using NOOK Study Apps on PC and Mac

NOOK Study is an app for the laptop or desktop developed by Barnes & Noble for reading and marking textbooks while at the same time prepping for tests, papers, and so on. Although intended for students, the NOOK Study app is a useful, feature-rich program, especially for Mac users, because the B&N eReader app for Mac lacks many features. For example, the NOOK Study app for the Mac includes syncing with your online library and reading of books that, at the Barnes & Noble store, are noted as "not readable on the Mac or Blackberry apps." For PC users, you do not need both apps, though having both doesn't cause any problems.

Following are the feature highlights. (The NOOK Study app for both the PC and Mac are essentially identical, so the focus is on the PC version for the rest of this section.)

▶ Syncing with your online library.

▶ Viewing multiple books at once and dual-book view.

▶ Customizable courses, which is a fancy way to say, "You can organize your books into categories."

▶ Enhanced note and lookup features.

These are covered while looking at the program.

Downloading, Installing, and Setting Up the NOOK Study App

To use this software, you need an Adobe Digital Editions (ADE) account. Go to adobe.com/products/digitaleditions/ to create one if you do not already have one.

You can find the NOOK Study app at barnesandnoble.com/nookstudy/download/index.asp. Download the appropriate version for your operating system. After the file has downloaded to your computer, double-click the file, and follow the instructions.

> NOTE: On the Mac, you first need to unzip the file. Then double-click the setup file.

After NOOK Study has installed, start the program. When you first start it, you are asked to agree to the License Agreement. Click Agree. You are then asked to enter your B&N account information. (This is the same account you use to purchase books on BN.com.) You can also create an account by clicking Create Account. If you have an account, click I Have an Account, and enter the account information. Next, enter your Adobe ID and password. Finally, enter your school. That's it! You are now ready to use NOOK Study.

> NOTE: If you are not a student and just want to use NOOK Study (particularly for Mac users), enter a school near you. I, so far, have not been able to gauge any effect on how the school matters.

Navigating NOOK Study

When you open NOOK Study (see Figure 18.24), it syncs with your My NOOK Library, so if you were on page 400 of *Moby-Dick* on your NOOK for iPhone app, when you open *Moby-Dick* on NOOK Study, it opens at page 400.

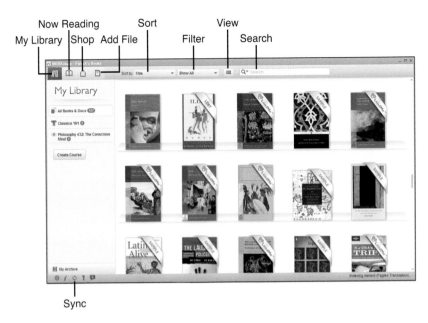

Now Reading   Sort   View

My Library Shop Add File   Filter   Search

Sync

FIGURE 18.24   The My Library screen.

Unlike the NOOK App for PC, there is no My Library, Shop, and such buttons. Instead, your library is shown. At the top of the screen, you have four buttons:

▶ **Library**: Clicking this takes you to your library.

▶ **Now Reading**: Clicking this takes you to the reading pane, where all ebooks you have open appear in tabs (much like the omnipresent browser tabs).

▶ **Shop**: Clicking this takes you to a link to purchase eTextbooks.

▶ **Add File**: Clicking this enables you to add PDFs and other ebooks.

These four buttons are always present and available.

Navigating NOOK Study's My Library View

While at the My Library screen, choose to see all your books and documents. You can also choose a particular course, which filters your viewing list to just books in that course. If you haven't yet done so, you can create a course. To create a course

1. Click Create Course. The Create a Course dialog box appears.

2. Give the course a name.

3. By default, for Course Icon, None is selected. Just click None or the drop-down arrow next to it to see a list of icons. Choose any that you like. (You'll notice these are thematic according to probable types of courses: Law, Science, Economics, Classics, and so on.)

4. Click Yes, Create Course. The course name and icon are added below the All Books & Docs option.

5. You can now select books from your library and drag them to the course to add books to that course. Note, doing this does not remove them from the All Books & Docs view.

After you finish with the course or if you need to make changes at any point in time, this is easy to do:

1. Click the course name. When you do this, you see two options: Edit and Delete.

2. Click Delete to delete the course. NOOK Study asks you to confirm that you want to delete the course. You are not deleting the books from your library, just deleting that particular course.

3. Click Edit to edit the name or icon for the course. The Edit Course Details dialog box appears.

4. This dialog box functions exactly as the Create a Course dialog box. After you have made your changes, click Proceed. Clicking Cancel dismisses the dialog box without implementing your changes.

You have a few more options on this screen. You can choose to view your Archived Books & Docs. From here, you can unarchive books or documents.

The Sync button forces a sync with My NOOK Library, which means that the existing page you were reading is sent to your library. When you next open your NOOK for iPad app or NOOK Color, you will be taken to that same page.

For some book purchases, you will be given an access code. Open NOOK Study, and click Redeem. Enter the access code here to get your eTextbook.

Clicking Settings enables you to modify your account information or unregister this instance of NOOK Study, which has the effect of removing your Barnes & Noble library from visibility and use.

Notifications indicates if you have loan offers for your review.

In the view of your books, you see some features similar to the NOOK for PC app. You can choose to Sort your books by Title, Author, Last Read, Note Count, or Recently Added.

You can also choose what type of books and documents you are looking at in this view by choosing the Filter drop-down list. Your options here are Show All, eBooks, eTextbooks, eNewspapers, eMagazines, and My Stuff.

You use the Search box to search the entire contents of your NOOK Study library. If I type **conscious**, NOOK Study searches for that word in all titles, notes, and text (see Figure 18.25). If you click the down arrow in the Search box, you can filter the results. For example, if I turn off the checkmark next to Title, Author, ISBN, NOOK Study does not search those items. Clicking the Matches Found next to the title displays the results in detail where the search term was found in that particular book. Click the specific result to go to that page in the book.

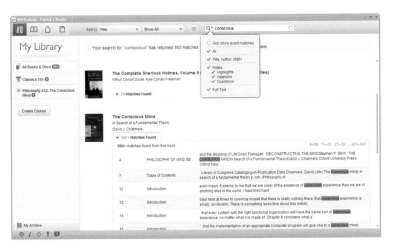

FIGURE 18.25   NOOK Study searches not only the titles, but the notes you've added and the full text.

You can also choose to see your books in either grid or list view. In grid view, clicking the book cover opens the books for reading. If you have not downloaded the book yet, it will download first. If you hover your mouse over the cover, you can see a plus sign in the bottom-right corner of the cover. Clicking it gives you a variety of options depending on if you have downloaded the ebook or issue, added notes, etc. (see Figure 18.26). If you haven't downloaded the book yet, you are also given an option to download the book.

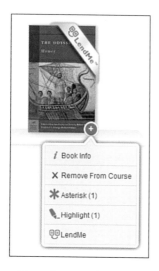

FIGURE 18.26 Click the plus sign on the cover to see available options.

Book Info is straightforward (see Figure 18.27): It takes you to a page with some information about the book along with options to Read Now, Download, Remove the Local Copy, and Archive it (or unarchive it if you have archived it). Click Go Back to go back to My Library. If you have added notes to the ebook, when you click the plus sign, you see a list of links for the type of notes you have made. Clicking one of types of notes opens the ebook with the Notes view open, which is discussed in the section "Using the Highlights, Notes, and Look Up Features of NOOK Study."

FIGURE 18.27 The Book Info screen.

In list view, clicking the cover image opens the book for reading. The Book Info link takes you to the Book Info page that is the same as what you get from the grid view. The notes links function the same as the notes links in the grid view.

> NOTE: For subscription content, instead of Book Info, you see Subscription Info. That screen let's you download, archive, and remove specific issues.

Reading Your Books in NOOK Study

Clicking the Now Reading button or a book cover takes you to the reading view (see Figure 18.28). Although initial impressions may be that this functions the same as the reading view in the NOOK App for PC, that impression will quickly disappear when you see the variety of options you have available.

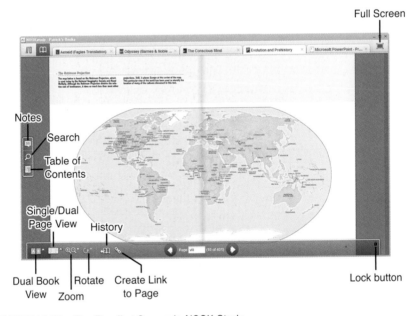

FIGURE 18.28   The Reading Screen in NOOK Study.

First and foremost, you can have multiple books open at once and navigate between them by clicking the tabs. Beyond that you have a host of buttons and options to explore, so dive into those features:

Dual Book View

You can look at books side by side to compare. Say you wanted to compare the Latin and English versions of *The Aeneid*. Easy.

1. Open one of the books, and then click the Dual Book button. The Dual Book View screen appears (see Figure 18.29).

FIGURE 18.29   Select the other book to read in dual book view.

2. You can either click From the Same Book to view side-by-side contents of the same book. Or you can click From a Different Book.

3. Assuming the latter in the previous step, you can scroll through your books until you find the one you want to open or use the search field to narrow that list. Click the book you want to open side by side.

> NOTE: The second book you want to open cannot already be open. If it is, close it first.

4. The second book opens and you get two reading screens, both with the same options (see Figure 18.30). The book that you are *in* (that is, the one where if you press the arrow key to turn the page, the page turns) has a large green arrow in the upper-left corner of that book's reading screen.

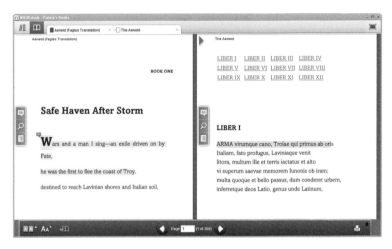

FIGURE 18.30   Reading two books side by side.

When you finish looking at the books in Dual Book view, click the Dual Book View button. You can close the left one, the right one, or split into single books. This last option changes the screen to appear as if you had opened each book individually into tabs.

Font

Click the Font button to adjust the font and font size for the book.

Page Turning

You can click the page right or page left buttons to turn the page (or use the arrow keys on your keyboard). Or you can enter the page number text box and type a specific page number.

Lock

The tiny Padlock icon on the far bottom right enables visibility of the bottom pane. Clicking it locks it so that it is always visible. Unlocking it changes the behavior so that the bottom pane drops out of view when you move the mouse cursor. To see the bottom pane, just drop the mouse cursor down.

My Notes View

Click this to open a screen on the left side of the reading screen to see the notes for this ebook (see Figure 18.31). The notes and highlights are presented in tabular format. The Type column indicates the type of note (Highlight, Asterisk, or Question). The Page column provides the page number of the note.

FIGURE 18.31   Viewing notes while in the Reading screen.

> NOTE: For more about entering notes and highlights and the associated options, **see** "Using the Highlights, Notes, and Look Up Features of NOOK Study."

> TIP: For the Type, Page, Added, and Tag columns, if you click the column header, you can sort the table based on that column's information.

The Note column provides the text of the note. The Date Added column provides the date the note was added. The Tag column lists any associated tags you indicated in the note. Clicking the individual notes displays the note on the page and provides note details.

Clicking Back to Reading hides this notes screen. Click Export to export the notes out to a Word or text document. You can also search for specific content in the notes by entering search criteria.

Full Screen Mode

Click this to open the book to take up the entire screen. Press Esc to close full screen mode.

Find

Use this button to search for a word or phrase in the ebook.

Table of Contents

Clicking this displays a table of contents for quick navigation to specific parts of the ebook (see Figure 18.32).

FIGURE 18.32   Navigating the table of contents while in the Reading screen.

Using the Highlights, Notes, and Look Up Features of NOOK Study

Adding notes and highlights to ebooks in NOOK Study is easy, and you have a variety of options. To add a highlight, follow these steps:

1. With the ebook open, select the text you want to highlight with the cursor. A pop-up menu appears (see Figure 18.33).

2. Click Apply Markup. You can choose Highlight, Asterisk, or Question from the menu. Other than using them for three different types of highlighting, the distinction is the icon used:

    Highlight: No icon

    Asterisk: Asterisk icon

    Question: Question mark icon

FIGURE 18.33 Text selection tools.

To add a note, follow these steps:

1. With the ebook open, select the text you want to highlight with the cursor. A pop-up menu appears.

2. Click Add Note. The Add Note dialog box appears (see Figure 18.34).

FIGURE 18.34 The Add Note dialog box.

3. Set the Markup Style to Highlight, Asterisk, or Question.

4. Enter the text of your note.

5. Add tags if you want them.

> NOTE: Tags can be useful for identifying notes with a similar type or theme. These can then come in handy if searching notes.

6. Add a hyperlink to outside research or articles. Click Add Link.

7. Click Save.

You can always edit the note by clicking the note in the reading screen.

NOOK Study also provides some look-up features. Just like creating a note, select the text you want to perform a search on at one of five websites:

- ▶ Dictionary.com

- ▶ Google

- ▶ YouTube

- ▶ Wikipedia

- ▶ Wolfram Alpha

The final option you have after you select text is Create Link to Selection. You can paste the created link into a research paper for reference.

Zooming and Rotating Books

With eTextbooks (versus NOOK Books), you can rotate and zoom in and out (see Figures 18.35 and 18.36). Click the Rotate and Zoom buttons respectively. The Rotate button basically gives you the option to view the book in landscape or portrait mode.

Using LendMe in NOOK Study

With NOOK Study, you can use B&N's LendMe feature. You can access the LendMe options, assuming LendMe is available for that NOOK Book, either from the plus sign menu or the Book Info screen. Clicking LendMe in either location opens the LendMe dialog box (see Figure 18.37).

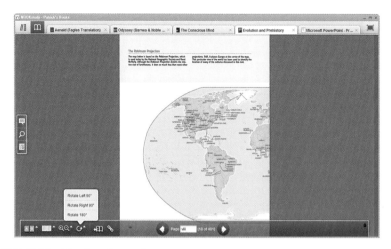

FIGURE 18.35 The Rotation options.

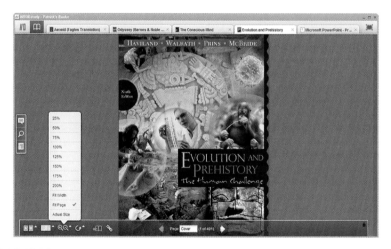

FIGURE 18.36 The Zoom options.

Enter the email address of the person you want to lend the NOOK Book to, enter a personal message if you want, and click Send.

The normal LendMe rules apply.

FIGURE 18.37   NOOK Study's LendMe dialog box.

Using Print to NOOK Study

Have a PowerPoint or Word document you want to add to your NOOK Study library? If so, it's easy. When you installed NOOK Study, it placed a print driver on your computer. So, if you are in PowerPoint or another program and you want to add that file to your NOOK Study library, choose File, Print. In your printer options, choose Print to NOOK Study (see Figure 18.38). (On the Mac, choose PDF down in the bottom left and click Print to NOOK Study from there.) Click Print. The file is automatically placed into your NOOK Study library.

Shopping with NOOK Study

You can shop for eTextbooks within NOOK Study. Click the Shop button. If you know the ISBN, you can enter that or enter keywords. When you click Search now, your browser opens at BN.com with the search results already in place.

Adding Your Own Files to NOOK Study

If you have a PDF or ePub file you want to add to NOOK Study, click Add File, navigate to the file, and click Open. The file is added to your library and you can manipulate it like any other document.

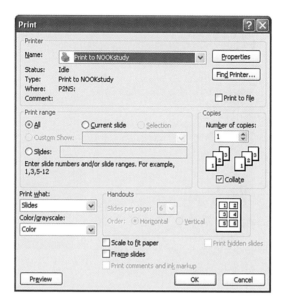

FIGURE 18.38   Printing to NOOK Study in PowerPoint.

Using the NOOK for Kids App for Your iPad

When the Barnes and Noble NOOK Color was released on November 19, 2010, one of its signature features was NOOK Kids Read to Me ebooks. These books featured a narration (and not a fake, mechanical-sounding one) if you wanted it. Moving from page to page, a child could hear the words read to them, and tapping the text would re-read that particular segment. Thumbnail views of each page mimicked the visual magazine representation. The downside of these books is that they were only available for the NOOK Color.

Fortunately, Barnes and Noble has recently released the NOOK for Kids app for iPad, which enables the same experience with NOOK Kids Read to Me ebooks whether you have a NOOK Color or an iPad.

Installing and Setting Up NOOK Kids for Your iPad

First, find the NOOK Kids app in iTunes, whether on your computer or on the iPad itself (in that case, use the App Store)—see Figure 18.39.

FIGURE 18.39　The NOOK Kids app in the iTunes store.

Once you have found the app, install it. If you downloaded it via iTunes, synch your iPad to load the app. With your iPad on, tap the NOOK Kids app icon.

The first time you start the app, you will be asked to enter your Barnes & Noble account information and name the library (for example, Aidan's Library)—see Figure 18.40.

You are ready to start browsing and reading NOOK Books.

Browsing Your B&N Library

After you have installed the NOOK for Kids app and so long as you are connected via wi-fi or 3G, your B&N NOOK Books library will appear on the shelves (see Figure 18.41). Anything that is a NOOK Kids Read to Me ebook and NOOK Book for kids (that is, ones without the Read to Me feature but "traditional" like *Curious George Goes to the Ice Cream Shop*). You may also notice NOOK Books that don't fit these categories directly: *The Adventures of Tom Sawyer* or *Grimm's Fairy Tales*. I have been unable to discern why those appear but others do not. No matter, you will be able to control which titles you want to appear in the NOOK Kids app (**see** "Using the Shop and Parents Button," later).

NOTE: Double-check on BN.com when you purchase kids books that it says Read to Me if you want the Read to Me feature.

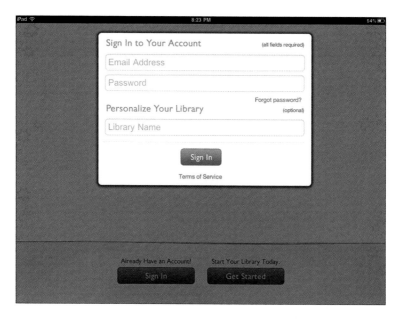

FIGURE 18.40   Enter your account information to start.

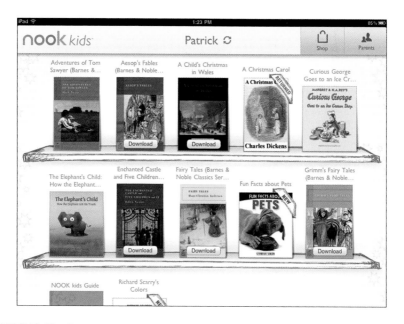

FIGURE 18.41   Browsing the library.

To download the book to your iPad so that you can read it, tap the Download button. You can tap the red x button to stop the download if you like (see Figure 18.42).

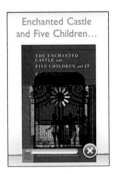

FIGURE 18.42   Downloading a NOOK Book.

To scroll up and down in your library, just press the screen and while holding your finger to the screen drag your finger up or down.

If you tap the Refresh button, any new purchases will appear or archived items will disappear.

You have two other options here: Shop and Parents. We'll cover these later in the "Using the Shop and Parents Button" section.

Reading a NOOK Kids ebook

To open a book, tap the book's cover in the library. Essentially, there are two types of books that you are read in NOOK for Kids app: Your traditional young children's book with a focus on images as well as text, and more straightforward texts, like *The Adventures of Tom Sawyer*. We'll cover both here, but let's focus first on the former.

Reading NOOK Books for Kids

These books, such as *The Elephant's Child: How the Elephant Got His Trunk*, always open and are read in landscape view (i.e., wider rather than taller). Many of these books have the Read to Me feature available (these books are labeled as NOOK Kids Read to Me on BN.com).

When you open these types of books, you are presented with two options: Read by Myself and Read to Me (see Figure 18.43). If the book is not a NOOK Kids Read to Me book, then you only have the option Read by Myself. Read by Myself means just that: No audio reading of the book will happen.

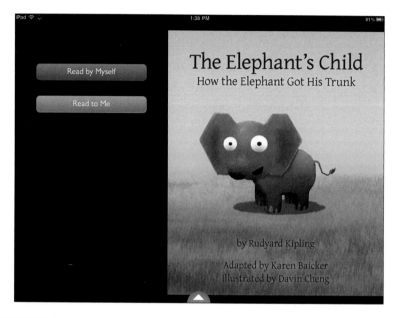

FIGURE 18.43 The opening page for a NOOK Kids Read to Me ebook.

If you choose Read to Me, as you advance from page to page, you will hear a person reading the text to you. You can pause the text and you can replay the text. If you do not make a choice and flip to the first page of the book, the default is Read to Me.

The basics are this: To advance a page, swipe the screen from right to left. To go back to a previous page, swipe the screen from left to right. Double-tapping the text places the text in a balloon, and you have a play button at the corner of the text (see Figure 18.44). Tapping this play button reads that portion of the text. If the button has a square in it, tapping that pauses the reading. If you chose Read to Myself, you can double-tap the text and press the play button to have it read the recording to you.

If the book is not a Read to Me book, if you double-tap the text, it is shown in a balloon without the play or pause button.

Using the Reading Options

As you read these books, you will notice a downward arrow button at the bottom of the page. If you tap this, a variety of reading options appears at the bottom of the page and thumbnails of the pages appear (see Figure 18.45).

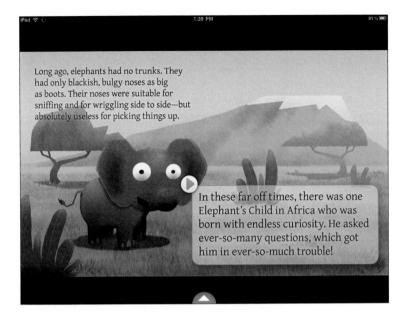

FIGURE 18.44 You can replay specific portions of the text.

FIGURE 18.45 Options available while reading.

▶ **Library**: Tap Library to go back to your B&N library.

▶ **Play/Pause**: Plays or pauses the reading for that page. If you chose Read to Myself, this option does not appear here (but you can double-tap the text and choose the play button to play the recording).

▶ **Pages**: Tap this to hide the thumbnails if they are visible or show them if they are hidden.

▶ **Brightness**: Adjust the brightness of the screen.

▶ **Thumbnails**: The current page you are on is marked with a blue outline. Press, hold, and drag the thumbnails back and forth to scroll through them. Tap a thumbnail to advance to that page. As you scroll, you will see a small light grey bar increase or decrease as you advance or retreat through the thumbnails. This is an indication of your overall location in the book.

Reading NOOK Books

These books, such as *The Adventures of Tom Sawyer*, open in either landscape or portrait mode. When there, to move to the next page, swipe your finger from right to left. To move to the previous page, swipe your finger from left to right. The reading screen, however, offers more options than just reading (see Figure 18.46).

If you do not see the surrounding bars in the reading screen, just tap the page and they will appear. Before exploring some of these options, take a quick tour:

▶ **Library**: Tapping this returns you to your NOOK library.

▶ **Go To**: Tapping this opens the table of contents with links to see your notes and annotations and bookmarks. You can scroll through any of these items and click the appropriate link to go quickly to that spot in the ebook.

▶ **Bookmark**: Tapping this adds a bookmark to this page.

▶ **Search**: Tapping this lets you search for specific text in this ebook.

▶ **Brightness**: Tapping this lets you adjust the brightness.

▶ **Font**: Tapping this allows you to adjust the specific font, justification, colors, and font size.

▶ **Scroll Bar**: Tapping and holding this lets you move quickly from page to page.

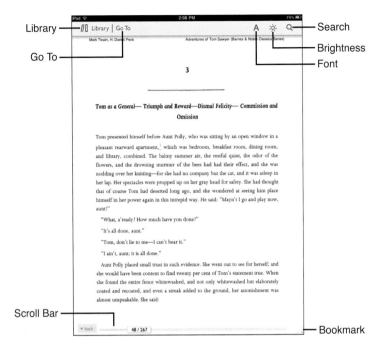

FIGURE 18.46 Options when reading regular NOOK Books.

Adjusting Fonts

After tapping Fonts, you see a screen like Figure 18.47.

The general purpose of this screen is to provide settings related to the reading experience in the NOOK App for regular NOOK Books. Tapping outside the Fonts screen closes it, returns you to the reading screen, and makes any changes that you have indicated.

Tapping Change Themes changes the screen, which really means text color, background color, and highlight color. You have five themes you can choose from. Tap the theme and either tap Back to adjust more font items or touch the reading screen.

Back at the Fonts screen, you can choose Use Publisher Settings. In an ebook, the publisher often provides a series of defaults (font size, type of font, and so on). Changing this option to On sets the settings to those publisher default settings. You can change it to Off at any time you want.

Tapping the A icon adjusts the font size. The current font size has an underline beneath it.

FIGURE 18.47   The font options when reading regular NOOK Books.

The set of icons beneath the font size determines line spacing. Think of this like single space, double space, and so on. The current setting has a line beneath that icon.

The Full Justification setting is either On or Off (and is Off by default). I have yet to see any difference in the reading screen with this option On or Off.

Depending on what the publisher of this ebook allows, you can adjust the font. You can scroll through the available list. (A check mark appears to the right of the currently selected one.) You have options between serif and sans serif fonts. What is this? Serif is a technical term that refers to the "hanging structure" on a letter. In Figure 18.47, if you look at the A icons, notice the little base at the bottom of each leg of the A? That's a serif. Sans (French for "without") serif fonts lack these structures. In general, most people find reading serif fonts easier on the eyes.

NOTE: Of the available font options, Amasis, Century Schoolbook, Georgia, Joanna, and Times New Roman are serif fonts. Ascender Sans, Gill Sans, and Trebuchet MS are sans serif fonts.

Adding Notes and Highlights in the NOOK for iPad App

Adding Notes, Highlights, and Bookmarks in the NOOK for iPad app is as easy as using your finger to select the part of the ebook you want to add a note or whatever to. Here's how you do it:

1. Using your finger, press and hold until you see the word your finger is on become highlighted; then select the text you want to add a Note or Highlight to. (If you just want that word, you can lift your finger.) The text will be highlighted according to the Font settings' Highlight color. As soon as you lift your finger from the selection, the Note & Highlights screen opens (see Figure 18.48).

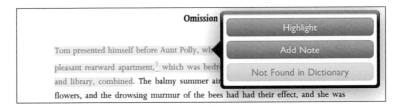

FIGURE 18.48   Adding a note or highlight.

2. Tap Highlight to add the highlight and nothing else.

   Tap Add Note to be taken to the Add Notes screen, where you can type in a note and tap Save Note.

   If you selected a single word, the Search Dictionary is an available option. Tapping it brings up a dictionary entry for the word. Tapping outside the definition screen takes you back to the reading screen.

3. The note and highlights are available for easy access using the Go To menu from the reading screen.

Using the Go To Menu

Speaking of the Go To menu, you use this menu to access the NOOK Book's table of contents or any note and highlights you have added.

While reading a NOOK Book, tap Go To to access the table of contents (see Figure 18.49). Tap any location in the table of contents to go to that spot in the NOOK Book.

FIGURE 18.49   Adding a note or highlight.

Tap Notes & Highlights or Bookmarks to access any of these that you have added to the NOOK Book. Tap the specific one you want to go to.

Using the Shop and Parents Button

We need to explore the final areas of the NOOK for Kids iPad app: Shop and Parents.

The shop piece is super easy, for tapping Shop asks for your password. Once you've entered it, the Safari browser opens on the NOOK Kids BN.com web page. From here on out, you can purchase ebooks just like you normally do via the B&N web page.

The Parents options provide a way to limit which books appear in the library and control password access. Tapping Parents first asks you to enter your password. You see a new screen that defaults to the Manage Kids' Library section (see Figure 18.50).

On this screen, you can control which books appear in the library and stored on the iPad. For example, if you want to allow *The Aeneid* to be read in the NOOK for Kids iPad app, you can tap the checkbox in the Show in Kids' Library column.

FIGURE 18.50   The Manage Kids' Library screen.

If you want to remove a book from the library in the NOOK for Kids app, you can tap the checkbox so that the checkmark no longer appears. Additionally, you can tap Remove to remove the file from the app (you can always re-add it by downloading it again).

When you tap Settings, you get the Settings screen (see Figure 18.51).

If you choose Save Parent Password, anyone accessing the Shop or Parents button does not need to enter a password. If you choose to not save the password (by removing the checkmark), anytime someone taps the Shop or Parents button they are required to enter the password. In other words, if you don't want your kids to control what ebooks appear in the Library, do not save the password.

Also here you can change the Library Name.

As you can tell, the NOOK for Kids app for iPad is an easy to use app, but it allows you to use the Read to Me features for kids books, whether you have a NOOK Color or not.

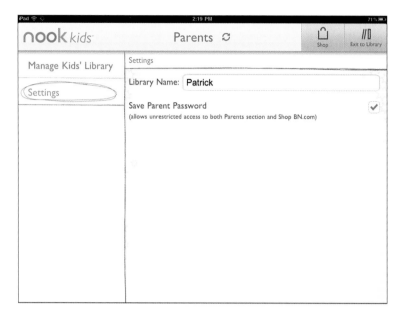

FIGURE 18.51   The Settings screen.

CHAPTER 19

Managing Your ebooks with Calibre

I have a huge library of ebooks. Because I get my ebooks from many different sources, they are spread out all over my hard drive. My ADE books are in one folder, books I've bought from Kobo are in another folder, and so on. All my files on my computer are backed up, so I'm not concerned about losing them, but it sure is easier to manage them when they are all in one location.

A while back, I discovered Calibre, a free application for managing an ebook library. Calibre is incredibly powerful, but it's also easy to use. In this chapter, you learn to use Calibre to manage your library, edit the metadata for your ebooks so they show up correctly on your NOOK Color and NOOK, get cover art when covers are missing, and sideload books to your NOOK Color and NOOK quickly and easily.

Configuring Calibre

You can download Calibre from calibre-ebook.com. There's a version for practically every type of computer on the market today. After you install Calibre, you need to specify a location for your Calibre library. When you add books to Calibre, it copies the ebook to your Calibre library. That way, all your ebooks are kept in one location.

To set up your Calibre library, simply launch Calibre, and it starts the Welcome Wizard. In the first step of the wizard, specify where you want Calibre to store your ebooks. You can choose any disk location you want, or you can leave it at the default setting.

Is There Any Advantage to Using a Custom Location for My Calibre Library?

In some situations, yes. For example, if you keep all your ebooks on your Windows Home Server, when you add a new ebook to your Calibre library, you may want Calibre to automatically copy the ebook to Windows Home Server, so you can specify your Calibre library on your Windows Home Server.

It might be better to say that there's no disadvantage to using a custom location for your Calibre library unless the location you specify is a network location you don't always have access to.

In the next step of the Welcome Wizard, select Barnes & Noble from the list of manufacturers and then select Nook from the list of devices. (Don't worry if you have a NOOK Color because Calibre treats both as a generic Nook.) Calibre uses your choice here for the default conversion settings. In other words, because you are choosing a NOOK as your reading device, Calibre knows it needs to convert ebooks to EPUB format when it sideloads ebooks onto your NOOK.

In the final step of the Welcome Wizard, Calibre displays links for tutorial videos and the Calibre user's guide. The videos are an excellent way to learn all the features of Calibre, but if you just want information you need to manage your library and sideload ebooks onto your NOOK Color or NOOK, you can skip them for now. (You can also access them at calibre-ebook.com/help.)

Adding Books to Your Calibre Library

When you first start using Calibre, your library is empty. To add books to your library, click the Add Books button on the toolbar. Select the books you want to add, and then click Open.

TIP: You can select multiple ebooks before you click Open; all the ebooks you select are added to your Calibre library.

Can I Add NOOK Books I've Purchased for My NOOK Color or NOOK to My Calibre Library?

Absolutely! Although Calibre does not allow you to read books protected by DRM, you can manage protected books with Calibre. That includes managing the book's metadata and adding a cover graphic.

When adding ebooks protected with DRM, you need to make sure that they are in either eReader or EPUB format. However, unprotected ebooks can be in any format. When you sideload unprotected ebooks to your NOOK Color or NOOK, Calibre automatically converts them into the correct format.

NOTE: If you use a NOOK Color, it cannot read eReader (PDB) formatted ebooks. Those books need to be converted to EPUB format, which you *cannot* do if they are secure eReader files.

Editing Metadata

As you add books to your library (see Figure 19.1), you might notice that some books have missing or incorrect metadata. For example, the book's title might not be formatted correctly or the listing in Calibre might be missing the author's name. You can edit the information Calibre uses for the book's listing by editing the book's metadata. You'll almost certainly want to be sure that your metadata is correct for all your ebooks because your NOOK Color and NOOK also uses metadata to display information about the ebooks.

FIGURE 19.1 The Calibre main window.

To edit metadata for an ebook, first select the ebook in Calibre, and then click Edit Metadata on the toolbar. Calibre displays the current metadata for the book you selected (see Figure 19.2). At this point, you can manually change the metadata or let Calibre retrieve metadata from either Google or ISBNdb.com.

To let Calibre automatically retrieve metadata for your ebook, click the Fetch Metadata from the Server button at the bottom of the Edit Meta Information dialog. Calibre uses the metadata shown in the dialog box to attempt a lookup on the book. If the metadata that already exists isn't sufficient, Calibre lets you know.

TIP: If Calibre cannot retrieve metadata for a particular book, enter the ISBN number (you can usually get it from BN.com or Amazon) for the book and try again. I've never experienced a problem when the ISBN number was entered first.

FIGURE 19.2   The Calibre Metadata Information screen.

By default, Calibre searches only Google for metadata. In most cases, Google has the metadata you need, but if it doesn't, you can also use ISBNdb.com as mentioned previously. To use ISBNdb.com, you need to sign up for a free account at ISBNdb.com/account. After you create your account, you must generate an access key that you can use in Calibre to authorize it to use ISBNdb.com. Here's how you do that:

1. Create an account at ISBNdb.com/account.

2. After you create your account, click Developer Area in the upper-left corner of the page.

3. Click the Manage Access Keys link.

4. Click Generate a New Key.

5. Enter a comment for your key. I entered "Calibre" so I know that's what this key is for.

6. Leave the Daily Use Limit blank, which sets the limit to unlimited.

7. Click the Generate New Key button to generate your key.

After you generate your key, copy it to your Clipboard. Switch over to Calibre and click the Fetch Metadata from the Server button. Enter your access key in the textbox, and click Fetch. From then on, Calibre will look up metadata in both Google and ISBNdb.com.

NOTE: If it seems like too much work to create an ISBNdb.com account and generate a key, don't worry about it. Google almost always has complete metadata for most books.

TIP: If you need to edit the title or author of an ebook, you can double-click the title or author name (and other metadata as well) in the Calibre library, type the new information, and press Enter.

Adding Covers

Because books you sideload onto your NOOK are kept in My Documents, you can't browse them by cover. However, you can see the cover on the touchscreen while you're reading the book—assuming a cover image is available. Sideloaded books on your NOOK Color, however, do show the cover when you view them in the Library.

NOTE: Recall that sideloaded books and content are ebooks and documents you have from sources other than B&N (for example, Fictionwise, Project Gutenberg, and so on).

Calibre can download covers for your ebooks automatically. You can even add covers to ebooks protected with DRM from the B&N NOOK Store or from another ebook store.

The easiest way to flip through cover images for your ebooks is to enable browsing by covers in Calibre. Click the Browse by Covers button shown in Figure 19.3 to enable this feature. You can then click either side of the current cover to flip to another cover or use the arrow keys on your keyboard to flip through your covers. To return to full library view, click the Browse by Covers button again.

TIP: You can also browse ebooks by tags using the Browse by Tags button immediately to the right of the Browse by Covers button. Tags are part of the metadata for an ebook, so you can edit how an ebook is tagged by editing the metadata.

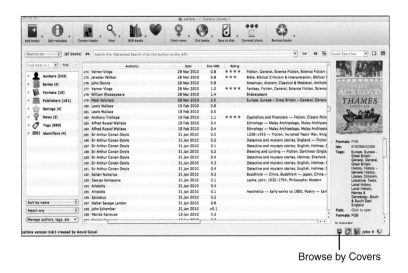

Browse by Covers

FIGURE 19.3   The Browse by Covers button makes locating missing covers much quicker.

To add (or replace) the cover image for an ebook, select the ebook and then click Edit Metadata. Click the Download Cover button at the bottom of the dialog box to add a cover image.

You can add cover images to multiple books by selecting more than one book in the Calibre library. On Windows, you can press Ctrl+A to select all your books. If you want to select multiple books that are listed contiguously, click the first book and then hold the Shift key, and click the last book. If you want to select multiple books that are not contiguous, click the first book; then hold the Ctrl key as you select the other books.

After you select all the books to which you'd like to add covers, click the down arrow to the right of the Edit Meta Information button, and select Download Only Covers from the menu. Calibre automatically downloads covers for all the books you selected.

Sideloading Books with Calibre

Sideloading books onto your NOOK Color or NOOK with Calibre is fast and easy. After you connect your NOOK to your computer, Calibre detects it and displays an icon for it in the area directly under the toolbar. If you have a microSD card installed in your NOOK Color or NOOK, Calibre displays an icon for both your NOOK Color and the microSD card.

NOTE: When you connect your NOOK Color or NOOK to a Windows computer, Windows assigns drive letters to your NOOK Color and to the microSD card if one is installed. Calibre assumes that the first drive letter assigned to your NOOK Color is its main memory and the second drive letter is the microSD card. However, sometimes Windows assigns the first drive letter to the microSD card; when it does that, Calibre incorrectly identifies your NOOK Color's main memory and the memory card.

To resolve this problem, you need to explicitly assign drive letters to your NOOK Color and its microSD card inside of Windows. For information on how to change drive letters in Windows, see www.online-tech-tips.com/computer-tips/how-to-change-the-drive-letter-in-windows-xp-for-an-external-usb-stick-or-hard-drive/.

TIP: Sometimes Calibre, if it is already open when you plug in your NOOK Color, won't recognize the NOOK Color as being installed. Close Calibre and restart it.

NOTE: At this point in time, Calibre treats the NOOK Color and NOOK as the same device, so the image for your NOOK Color in Calibre is the NOOK. This is cosmetic only, and Calibre correctly interacts with the NOOK Color or NOOK.

To sideload one or more books onto your NOOK Color, make sure your NOOK is connected to your computer. Select the books from your library, and click Send to Device on the toolbar. Calibre automatically converts any ebooks that are not already in a format compatible with your NOOK Color and then transfers them to your NOOK. By default, Calibre transfers ebooks to your NOOK Color's main memory, but you can choose to transfer them to the microSD card if you want. Simply click the down arrow next to the Send to Device button, and select Send to Storage Card A from the menu.

TIP: You can also select Set Default Send to Device Action and select Send to Storage Card A. From then on, clicking the Send to Device button automatically sideloads any selected ebooks to your NOOK's microSD card.

Depending on what action is necessary, Calibre might take a while to sideload books. Calibre indicates that it's working and how many jobs it's currently processing using the progress indicator in the lower-right corner of the main window. If you click the progress indicator, you can see details on what Calibre is doing.

If I Update Some Metadata Information for an ebook That's Already Sideloaded onto My NOOK Color and Sideload It onto My NOOK Color Again, Will It Overwrite the Existing Copy on My NOOK Color?

Yes. Both Calibre and your computer use the filename of an ebook to identify it as a unique ebook. If you change metadata information (such as the title, author, and so on) of an ebook that is already on your NOOK Color, sideloading it onto your NOOK Color will overwrite the existing copy. Essentially, you're just updating the metadata of the copy on your NOOK Color.

There is one exception to this. If you sideload an ebook to your NOOK Color's main memory and the same ebook is already on its microSD card, you will have a duplicate copy of the book and it will show up twice in your library.

Can I Read My ebooks Using Calibre?

You can read an ebook on your computer using Calibre as long as the ebook isn't protected with DRM. To read an ebook with Calibre, select the ebook, and click the View button on the toolbar.

Subscribing to News Content in Calibre

Calibre also has an excellent news subscription feature that makes it easy to subscribe to various news feeds that you can then sync to your NOOK Color. To access this feature, click the Fetch News button, select a news feed, and set the subscription options that determine how often the feed is downloaded. Keep in mind that for feeds to download, Calibre must be running.

TIP: I particularly like this feature (subscribing to news content in Calibre). I have print subscriptions to *The London Review of Books* and *The New York Review of Books*, which I paid for long before I got my NOOK Color. Although I could subscribe again to *The New York Review of Books* at BN.com, I would be paying for two subscriptions...so I use Calibre to fetch that news (using my account information from *The New York Review of Books* website). When my print subscription runs out, I will switch to the BN.com subscription...but for now, I only pay for one.

Calibre uses a collection of properties known as a "recipe" to subscribe to a particular news feed. If you don't see a news feed that you're interested in, you can find others and submit requests for new recipes by browsing to http://bugs.calibre-ebook.com/wiki/UserRecipes.

Converting ebooks in Calibre

Calibre can convert a wide variety of formats. Although your NOOK Color can read Word, PDF, HTML, and text documents, these are not treated as "real" ebooks by the NOOK Color. What that means is that you cannot add notes or highlights, bookmark pages, and so on. So although you can read those formats, you may want to convert them to the EPUB format so that they get the full ebook treatment.

Calibre's conversion options are rich, and I won't go into the details here. The standard default PDF to EPUB, HTML to EPUB, and such work quite well. To convert a document, follow these steps:

1. Add the document to your Calibre library if you haven't already.

2. Select the book you want to convert.

3. Click the Convert Books button.

4. Click OK.

If you want more details about the vast number of options for conversion, go to calibre-ebook.com/user_manual/conversion.html.

> NOTE: PDFs are the most problematic documents to convert because of the way they are created. So if the results are less than satisfactory, you might tweak some of the settings to see if you can get better results.

In this chapter, you've seen how powerful Calibre is for managing your ebook library. You've also seen how easily you can edit the metadata for your ebooks, add missing covers to your ebooks, and sideload ebooks onto your NOOK.

CHAPTER 20

Using My NOOK Library

All your B&N content is saved on the bn.com website in what B&N calls My NOOK Library. Using My NOOK Library, you can browse through your B&N content, lend and borrow books with LendMe, move items to and from your archive, and delete items from your B&N library.

Accessing My NOOK Library

You can access My NOOK Library by browsing to http://my.barnesandnoble.com/ ebooks/ebookslibrary.html. Two views are available in My NOOK Library: Full view (the default) and Reduced view. To switch between the two views, click one of the View buttons, as shown in Figure 20.1—the one that is colored green is the one not in use.

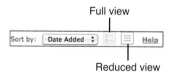

FIGURE 20.1   The View buttons enable you to choose between Full and Reduced view.

> NOTE: The only difference between Full and Reduced view is that covers display in Full view and are not in Reduced view.

By default, all items in your B&N online library that have not been archived are displayed in My NOOK Library. You can filter the view by clicking Books, Sample Books, Magazines, Newspapers, Apps, or eTextbooks on the left side of the page. You can also view any items that have been archived by clicking the Archive link.

To sort the items displayed in My NOOK Library, click the Sort By drop-down (refer to Figure 20.1) and select from one of the sorting options.

Archiving, Deleting, and Lending Books in My NOOK Library

You can easily delete or archive content in My NOOK Library. Archiving an item moves it to your archive, and you can move items from the archive back to the library by unarchiving them. On the other hand, deleted items are permanently removed from your library.

CAUTION: Be careful about deleting items. If you delete an item from your library, it will be removed from your NOOK Color and all other devices where you access your B&N content. The only way to get it back is to buy it again. Archiving is the safe bet.

If you have downloaded sample NOOK Books onto your NOOK Color or NOOK and you want to remove them, you must use My NOOK Library to do that. Locate the sample and click Delete to remove them from your library. After you removed them from your library, your NOOK Color updates. (Or you can force it to update by tapping Library from the Quick Nav Bar and then tapping the Sync button.) On your NOOK, open My B&N Library, and tap Check for New B&N Content to update your library.

To archive an item, click the Move to Archive link in My NOOK Library. The item is moved to your archive on your NOOK Color or NOOK as well. To move the item back to your library, click Archive on the left side of My NOOK Library; then click the Move to Library link for the item you want to move back to your library.

TIP: Think of My NOOK Library as another way that you can view your NOOK Book library on your NOOK Color or NOOK. When you interact with content via My NOOK Library, you also impact the content on your NOOK Color, NOOK, NOOK Apps, and NOOK Study.

Books that can be lent to friends using the LendMe feature are marked as such in My NOOK Library. To lend a book to a friend, click the LendMe logo and enter your friend's email address (see Figure 20.2). While the book is on loan, its cover displays a Lent badge notifying you that it cannot currently be read by you.

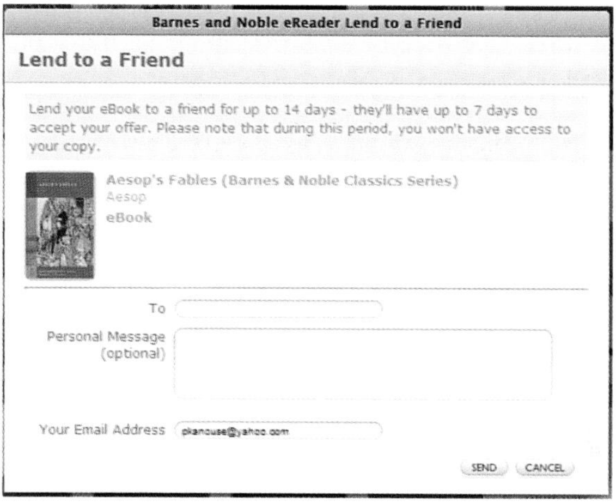

FIGURE 20.2 Lending a book from My NOOK Library.

Downloading Content from My NOOK Library

You can download NOOK Books and subscription content from My NOOK Library for reading on your computer or for local archival purposes. You can download items to your computer and then sideload them onto your NOOK Color or NOOK later. However, keep in mind that if you do this, the item will not show up in My B&N Library on your NOOK. Instead, it will show up in My Documents just like all other sideloaded content.

> NOTE: The only difference between Full and Reduced view is that covers display in Full view and are not in Reduced view.

When you download ebooks to your computer, you can then add them to your Calibre library. This is a convenient way to ensure that you have a backup of your B&N content in case you accidentally delete an item.

Can I Send an Item to My NOOK Color or NOOK from My NOOK Library?

There isn't a way that you can manually send an item to your NOOK Color or NOOK from My NOOK Library. However, because My NOOK Library is actually just another way to view your B&N online library, you should always see the same content on your NOOK Color, NOOK, NOOK Apps, or NOOK Study.

CHAPTER 21

Using PubIt to Sell Your ebooks

PubIt is a B&N feature that enables you to submit your ebook for sale through the B&N website. PubIt books are NOOK Books. When people visit BN.com and browse or search for ebooks, yours will be available. If they buy it, it downloads, can be lent, and can use the social features like any other NOOK Book.

Setting Up PubIt

Setting up and using PubIt is easy:

1. Go to http://pubit.barnesandnoble.com/pubit_app/bn?t=pi_reg_home.

2. Enter in your BN.com username and password and click Sign In or create one from here. The Account Setup screen appears.

3. For PubIt, B&N needs to set up a PubIt account though it uses your BN.com information. Update any information here.

4. Because you are publishing your work, provide a name and website if you want. Note: If you leave this blank, your first and last name will be used as the publisher. Click Continue. The Terms and Conditions page appears.

Important Information about PubIt Terms and Conditions

Normally you might just blindly click I Agree or Accept when you see the kind of legalese included in the PubIt Terms and Conditions, but it is important that you understand something about PubIt before you agree to this.

B&N can update the pricing and payment terms whenever it wants. At the time of this writing, you, the publisher, can set a price for your content anywhere from $.99 to $199.99. For books priced $2.99 to $9.99, the publisher receives a 65% royalty. For books priced from $.99 to $2.98 or from $10.00 to $199.99, the publisher receives 40%.

B&N also requires that the publisher comply with the Content Policy. So if B&N deems your content offensive, harmful, legally obscene, and so on, it can choose not to sell your content. It then provides some specific examples but certainly does not cover all areas.

You cannot include the following in the Product Data:

▶ Hyperlinks of any kind, including email addresses.

▶ Request for action (for example, "If you like this book, please write me a review.").

▶ Advertisements or promotional material (including author events, seminars, and so forth).

▶ Contact information for the author or publisher.

B&N will make your product available in the Read In and LendMe programs. Additionally, 5% of the book's content will be provided as a sample for people to download to their NOOK Color, and such, to try before they buy.

A whole lot of other information is in this agreement (covering such things as withdrawing a book from the PubIt program, book rejection and reformatting, and so on), so I highly recommend reading through all the legalese before agreeing. This is your content, so treat this document as what it is: a contract.

5. If you agree with these terms, click I agree and Continue. The Payment Information screen appears.

6. Enter Bank Account, Tax Information, and Credit Card Information and click Submit. A page appears indicating that your account is being set up.

Putting Content into PubIt

Now that your account is set up, load up your first title:

1. Click Add a Title (see Figure 21.1) and enter the required fields (see Figure 21.2).

2. To upload your ebook, click Browse, navigate to it, and click it. Click Upload & Preview. If the file you chose is not an EPUB file, B&N converts it to an EPUB file. Either way, you then see a virtual Nook with your text in it. Flip through pages to make sure you are satisfied with the appearance. If you need to tweak it, do so on the source file and then re-upload it.

3. Upload a cover in JPEG format between 750 and 2,000 pixels in length.

4. Enter the metadata info. Accurate and thorough metadata about the content, genre, and so on is important when visitors to BN.com search for a title. If your book is a spy eco-thriller taking place on the remote island of Tonga, you want to give potential buyers the best chance to find it.

FIGURE 21.1 The My Titles screen on Publt.

FIGURE 21.2 Setting up a new title to sell.

5. Click the I Confirm box, and then click Put on Sale. A window appears indicating a 24–72 hour timeframe for it be done (see Figure 21.3).

If you later want to adjust any of the information, from My Titles, click Actions, Edit. You can then modify the price, title, metadata, cover, and upload newer versions of the content.

FIGURE 21.3   Soon your ebook will be for sale!

NOTE: The first time you upload a document, it can take 48–72 hours for the item to be on sale. Subsequent updates tend to update much faster, usually within 4–8 hours.

If I Update My Book with a New File, Does It Automatically Get Sent to Customers Who Purchased My ebook?

If you update your ebook after it has gone on sale with a new version of the content, customers who have purchased the original version do *not* automatically receive the new version. However, if they delete the local copy on the device, when they redownload it, they receive the latest version available.

With the other tabs in the PubIt interface, you can watch your sales (including any royalties coming your way), adjust your account information, and get support.

TIP: If your child has a kids book idea, check out B&N Tikatok books at http://www.barnesandnoble.com/u/kids-activities-publish-a-childrens-book/379002382. Here, kids can create their own books that can be made into hardcover, softcover, or PDF.

Understanding ebook Formats

An Overview of ebook Formats

You can use the following types of ebooks on your NOOK Color:

- ▶ EPUB (including Adobe Digital Editions)
- ▶ PDF

> NOTE: That's right. If you purchased secure eReader (PDB) files from Fictionwise or eReader.com, your NOOK Color will not read those files. It is rumored that a future NOOKextra app will enable you to read PDB files from Fictionwise or eReader.com.

You can use the following types of ebooks on your NOOK:

- ▶ EPUB (including Adobe Digital Editions)
- ▶ eReader (PDB) from B&N and non-DRM eReader from third parties

> **Can I Read Word Documents or TXT Files on My NOOK Color or NOOK?**
>
> If you want to read Word documents or TXT files on your NOOK Color and treat them as ebooks versus Word documents, you need to first convert them into EPUB files.
>
> Calibre can convert TXT files to the EPUB format for your NOOK Color. If you want to read a Word document, it's best to save the file as a PDF file. (Recent versions of Word provide this functionality.) If you cannot save the Word document as a PDF, first save it as an HTML file, and then use Calibre to convert it for your NOOK Color.

For more information on using Calibre to convert ebooks, **see** Chapter 19, "Managing Your ebooks with Calibre."

EPUB Format

EPUB (electronic publication) is an open-source format for ebooks. That means the format isn't owned by any single entity, making it an ideal format for electronic books. EPUB ebooks have a file extension of .epub, but EPUB files are actually Zip files (a compressed collection of files) that contain content files for the book along with other supporting files that specify the formatting.

> NOTE: The EPUB format was created to replace the Open eBook format, a format that was widely used in the first ebook readers.

EPUB ebooks are actually just HTML files—just like the files used for web pages. The same technologies used in displaying web pages are used to display EPUB ebooks. If you rename an EPUB book and give it a .zip file extension, you can open the file and see all the files contained in the EPUB archive.

EPUB ebooks can be protected with *digital rights management* (*DRM*), which is designed to prevent unauthorized users from accessing digital content such as ebooks. When you purchase a book on your NOOK Color or from bn.com, that content is tied to your bn.com account using DRM. B&N uses its own DRM mechanism for books purchased from B&N, but your NOOK Color also supports Adobe Digital Editions DRM.

eReader Format

ebooks in the eReader format have a .pdb file extension. The eReader format was originally used for reading books on Palm PDAs. However, other ebook readers adopted the format as well.

> NOTE: The Stanza application for the iPhone, iPad, and iPod touch uses the eReader format.

The eReader format enables DRM using the purchaser's name and credit card number. Your NOOK Color cannot read DRM eReader files. If you want to read eReader files from third parties, you need to ensure that they do not contain DRM so that you can convert them to EPUB format.

For more information on sideloading content on your NOOK Color, **see** "Sideloading Books with Calibre" in Chapter 19.

Using Adobe Digital Editions

Adobe Digital Editions (ADE) is software that manages ebooks that use ADE DRM. Your NOOK Color and NOOK are compatible with ADE DRM and can be configured as an authorized device in the ADE software.

> NOTE: You can download ADE software free from adobe.com/products/digitaleditions/.

To authorize your NOOK Color or NOOK for ADE DRM, connect your NOOK Color or NOOK to your computer while ADE is running. When you do, you see a dialog box informing you that your NOOK Color or NOOK was detected and needs to be authorized (see Figure A.1). Click the Authorize Device button to authorize your NOOK Color or NOOK.

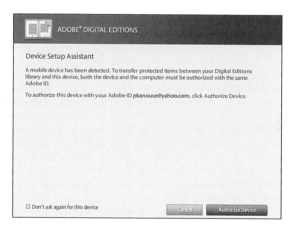

FIGURE A.1   Authorize your NOOK Color to use ADE ebooks.

> NOTE: Sometimes I have to connect the NOOK Color or NOOK first before starting ADE.

After your NOOK is authorized, ADE displays an icon for your NOOK Color or NOOK in the bookshelf on the left side of the main window. If you click that icon, you see all the content on your NOOK Color that is compatible with ADE. Any content in EPUB or PDF format is available for reading directly in ADE.

NOTE: ADE does not yet distinguish between the NOOK Color or NOOK. It simply refers to it as NOOK.

TIP: I have a few ADE books I have purchased that I could not read on my iPhone or iPad because apps such as Stanza, eReader, and others did not support ADE books. However, the Bluefire eReader app does support ADE, so check it out.

APPENDIX B

Sources for ebooks Other than B&N

EPUB Sources

You can buy EPUB books or download free EPUB books that you can read on your NOOK Color from numerous places. Here are just a few:

- ▶ Gutenberg.org
- ▶ Fictionwise (www.fictionwise.com)
- ▶ Feedbooks.com
- ▶ eBooks.com
- ▶ Smashwords (www.smashwords.com)
- ▶ BooksOnBoard (www.booksonboard.com)
- ▶ Kobo Books (www.kobobooks.com)
- ▶ Diesel eBook Store (www.diesel-ebooks.com)
- ▶ Powells.com
- ▶ Baen (www.baen.com)

Some of these sites offer ebooks in several formats, so be sure you select carefully and get the EPUB version.

Perhaps one of the greatest benefits to having an ebook reader that supports the EPUB format is that you can read ebooks from many public libraries. Check with your local library to see if it offers the capability of checking out EPUB ebooks. If it doesn't, you might still be able to get a library card from a nearby library. Check out the Overdrive website at www.overdrive.com. You can enter your ZIP code and it will give you a list of libraries in your area that support Overdrive for checking out EPUB books.

eReader Sources for Your NOOK

Following are a few sources for free, non-DRM eReader ebooks:

- Manybooks.net

- eReader.com

- Fictionwise.com

> TIP: Inkmesh.com and Ebooks.addall.com are ebook price comparison sites. Enter a title or author and see what Amazon, B&N, Fictionwise, Kobo, and others are charging for that ebook.

Use Calibre to Search for ebooks

In 2011, Calibre came out with a release that added an ebook search function. One of the great things about Calibre's feature is that you can control which locations to look at as well as get DRM status. Calibre does not let you purchase a book through them, but it can give you a quick look at what's available.

Open Calibre and click Get Books. The Get Books dialog opens (see Figure B.1).

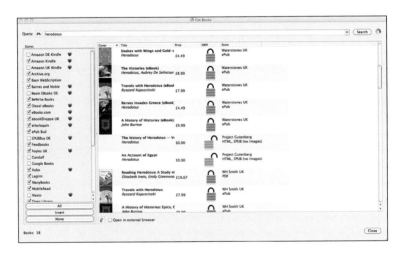

FIGURE B.1   Use Calibre to search for ebooks.

You can adjust which stores to search by clicking the appropriate checkboxes in the Store list. In the Query box, type your search criteria. Click Search.

If you double-click a title in the search results, Calibre opens that web page. Alternatively, you can click Open in External Browser, and when you double-click a title, your default browser opens to that web page. As usual, Calibre offers extensive settings options, so feel free to explore.

Libraries and ebooks

Many libraries offer selections of ebooks that you can read on your NOOK Color or NOOK. A popular ebook lending service for libraries is Overdrive. If you are curious if your library offers ebook lending services, go to http://www.overdrive.com/ and enter your ZIP code. A list of libraries appears. Select the link to your library to see what they have available.

To check out library ebooks, you first need to have a valid library card from that particular lending library. The specifics can be found at that library. Using the library's website, select the title you want. Most offerings from libraries are either PDF or EPUB, both of which you can read on your NOOK Color or NOOK.

Download the file as instructed by the library. Most of the time, you need to open the file using Adobe Digital Editions (**see** Appendix A's section, "Using Adobe Digital Editions," for information about using that software). You can then sideload the book to your NOOK Color or NOOK.

NOTE: Libraries have their own policies, guidelines, and requirements, so be sure to check all the available information on the library's website to understand the options related to ebook lending. You can also contact the library directly and speak to a librarian to get answers.

APPENDIX C

Sideloading Adobe Digital Editions

To sideload ADE content to your NOOK Color or NOOK (referenced as NOOK Color from here on), connect your NOOK Color to your computer, and launch ADE if it's not already running. Drag the ebook from your ADE library to the NOOK icon in the bookshelf.

ADE supports both protected PDF files and protected EPUB files.

> TIP: One of the most popular ebook stores for ADE books is ebooks.com.

When ADE books are copied to your NOOK Color, ADE creates a folder called Digital Editions, and the books are copied to this folder. Unlike protected books from eReader.com and Fictionwise, ADE ebooks don't require you to enter any information to open them. As long as your NOOK Color is an authorized device, you can open ADE EPUB books.

> TIP: When you sideload content onto your NOOK, you find the items in My Documents. You need to tap Check for New Content before the new item is visible in My Documents.

> NOTE: ADE does not yet distinguish between the NOOK Color or NOOK. It simply refers to it as NOOK.

You don't need to use ADE to sideload ADE EPUB books onto your NOOK Color. I prefer using Calibre to manage all my ebooks and use it to sideload ADE books onto my NOOK Color. See Chapter 19, "Managing Your ebooks with Calibre," for more information about Calibre.

Using Picasa to Create Wallpapers and Screensavers

Creating Wallpaper and Screensaver Images

Before you use a picture as wallpaper or a screensaver on your NOOK Color or NOOK, you need to resize it to fit the dimensions of the reading screen. For the NOOK Color, the wallpaper image needs to be at least 600x1024. However, if you want the scrolling wallpaper (where the image shifts slightly as you flip through the home pages), the size needs to be 768x1024.

For the NOOK, screensaver images need to be 800 pixels high and 600 pixels wide.

> TIP: I use Google's Picasa (www.picasa.com) to resize images for my NOOK Color and NOOK. It's a free program and is available for Windows, Macs, and Linux computers.

> TIP: Of course, on the NOOK Color, you can use the create wallpaper features. **See** Chapter 2, "Customizing and Configuring Your NOOK Color."

Many of your pictures are likely in landscape orientation. In other words, they are wider than they are tall. If you want to use a landscape-oriented picture as a screensaver on your NOOK, your best option is to crop the image. When you crop an image, you select part of the image to keep and discard the rest of the image.

Picasa enables you to create custom aspect ratios for use when cropping images. This feature enables you to quickly and easily crop images for use on your NOOK. To set up a custom aspect ratio in Picasa, follow these steps:

1. Locate the image you want to use, and double-click it to open it in the editor.

2. Select the Crop tool on the Basic Fixes tab in the panel on the left.

3. Click the dimension drop-down and select Add Custom Aspect Ratio.

4. In the Add Custom Aspect Ratio dialog, change the dimensions to 600 x 800.

5. Enter NOOK Screensaver in the Name textbox as shown in Figure D.1, and click OK.

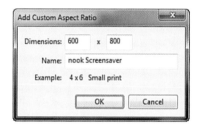

FIGURE D.1   A custom aspect ratio in Google Picasa.

After you set up these custom aspect ratios, you can simp ly select NOOK Screensaver from the dimension drop-down in Picasa to easily crop your image to the appropriate dimensions.

> TIP: When cropping your image, make sure that the cropped portion is taller than it is wide. If the cropped area looks almost square, move your mouse pointer left or right toward the center of the crop area; Picasa flips it to the taller orientation necessary for your NOOK.

Now consider a couple of important things about cropping in Picasa. First, you don't need to worry about ruining an important picture because Picasa performs all editing operations on a copy of the original image. Therefore, when you crop an image in Picasa, the original image remains unchanged.

Second, when you crop an image using one of your custom aspect ratios, Picasa doesn't actually resize the image to the dimensions necessary for your NOOK. Instead, it crops out an area that is the correct aspect ratio for your NOOK. To actually resize the image for your NOOK, you need to export the image. If you're still using the crop tool, apply your crop or click cancel first. After you do that, you can export the image for use on your NOOK by following these steps:

1. Select the image(s) you want to export for use on your NOOK. (If you're viewing a single image in the editor, you need to click Back to Library to select multiple images.)

2. Click the Export button at the bottom of the Picasa interface.

3. Choose a location for your exported images. Remember where you are exporting the images so that you can find them. (I find it easiest to export to my desktop.)

4. Select the Resize To option button, and enter 800 for screensaver images.

5. Click the Export button to export the image(s).

When you enter the size in step 4, you are actually specifying the height for the exported image. Picasa automatically adjusts the width to match the aspect ratio. If you cropped the image using the correct custom aspect ratio earlier, the final dimensions of the image will be perfect for your NOOK.

Can I Use Images for My Screensaver That Won't Properly Size to the Necessary Dimensions for My NOOK?

Yes. Your NOOK isn't picky about the size of the images you use. Your NOOK can resize images automatically to fit on its reading screen. However, if the aspect ratio of the image isn't correct, you see black bars at the top and bottom or left and right of the screen.

Remember that your images take up memory on your NOOK, so you should try to use the smallest file size possible. By resizing your images to the appropriate size, you can substantially reduce the size of the image file. That means less memory used on images and more free memory for your books!

The steps to get your exported images onto your NOOK differ depending on whether you use the images for a screensaver. Therefore, look at each process separately.

APPENDIX E

Can I Read This Here?

With all the devices available for reading NOOK Books, the following should help you distinguish which formats can be read on each device.

	NOOK Color	NOOK	NOOK for PC Mac App	NOOK for iPhone and Android™	NOOK for iPad	NOOK for Kids for iPad	B&N eReader Apps	NOOK Study
NOOK Books	Yes	Yes	Yes	Yes	Yes	Yes	Yes	Yes
NOOK Books for Kids with Read to Me	Yes	No	No	No	No	Yes	No	No
NOOK Books for Kids with Read and Play	Yes	No	No	No	No	No	No	No
eTextbooks	No	No	No	No	No	No	No	Yes
Newspapers	Yes	Yes	Yes	No	Yes	No	No	Yes
Magazines	Yes	Yes[1]	No	No	Yes[1]	No	No	No
Enhanced NOOK Books	Yes	No	No	No	Yes[1]	No	No	No
Supports LendMe	Yes	Yes	Yes	Yes	Yes	No	Yes[2]	Yes

[1] Some magazines are readable—check the magazine's product page at BN.com to verify.

[2] You must first download the file from My NOOK Library at BN.com.

APPENDIX F

Frequently Asked Questions

Questions Often Asked by NOOKies

Throughout this book, numerous questions are highlighted that I've seen from NOOKies. This appendix includes a list of all these questions and the page within the book where each question is answered.

1. Does my NOOK Color's/NOOK's battery drain faster with Wi-Fi connected? p. 5, 170

2. Should I plug my NOOK into a surge suppressor? p. 172

3. How should I clean my NOOK Color's/NOOK's touchscreen? p. 8, 172

4. Can I use images for my wallpaper or screensaver that won't properly size to the necessary dimensions for my NOOK? p. 297

5. Should I use a specific file format for images? p. 16, 173

6. If I don't like changes made by a firmware update, can I go back to an older version? p. 176

7. Can I use a high-capacity microSD card in my NOOK? p. 180

8. Can I read Word documents or TXT files on my NOOK? p. 181

9. How can I delete sideloaded content because there isn't a menu option for removing it? p. 48, 187

10. I want to lend a book to one of my friends. Does my friend have to own a NOOK Color/NOOK for me to lend her a book? p. 75, 195

11. If my friend finishes a loaned book before 14 days have elapsed, can she return the book to me immediately? p. 195

12. What happens if I lend my friend a book that she already owns? p. 194

13. Is it possible to accidentally purchase a book that I've already purchased from B&N's NOOK Store? p. 148, 207

14. Is it risky to root my NOOK Color? p. 157

15. Is there any advantage to using a custom location for my Calibre library? p. 267

16. Can I add NOOK Books I've purchased for my NOOK Color or NOOK to my Calibre library? p. 268

17. If I update some meta information for an ebook that's already sideloaded onto my NOOK Color and sideload it onto my NOOK Color again, will it overwrite the existing copy on my NOOK Color? p. 274

18. Can I read my ebooks using Calibre? p. 274

19. Can I send an item to my NOOK Color or NOOK from My NOOK Library? p. 279

20. If I update my PubIt book with a new file, does it automatically get sent to customers who purchased my ebook? p. 284

21. How do I find out if there are updates to my NOOK Apps? p. 100

You're now a NOOK expert. I hope you take all you've learned and use it to get the most out of this extraordinary device. Happy reading!

Index

D

E

J–K–L

M

Swipe Left/Swipe Right gestures, 1, 167
Synch button (Library), 182

T

table of contents in NOOK Study, 248
Tap gesture, 1, 167
terms and conditions for PubIt, 281-282
Text Selection toolbar
    Share option, 137-138
    sharing to Facebook, 203
text size, changing for NOOK Books
    on NOOK, 189
    on NOOK Color, 50-51
Time section/menu
    on NOOK, 177
    on NOOK Color, 21
time zone settings on NOOK, 177
touchscreen, cleaning
    on NOOK, 172
    on NOOK Color, 8
troubleshooting, lending ebooks, 194
Twitter
    linking to, 29, 178-179
    NOOK Color support for, 139
Twitter sharing, 203
TXT files
    converting for NOOK Color, 285
    reading on NOOK, 181
Type button (Library), 182-183

U-V

unarchiving Library items on NOOK, 186
Unpinch gesture, 1

unrooting NOOK Color, 164-165
updating firmware, 176
uploading content into PubIt, 282-284

version names (Android OS), 157-158
video files, playing on NOOK Color, 95-96. *See also* enhanced NOOK Books
View Details screen, Recommend option, 132-133
viewing
    bottom pane in NOOK Study, 246
    Daily with NOOK for PC app, 214
    item details on NOOK, 185, 187
    notes/highlights
        in NOOK, 198-199
        in NOOK Color, 84-85
        in NOOK for PC app, 217
visibility of LendMe books, 204
volume buttons on NOOK Color, 8

W-Z

wallpaper
    creating images for, 295-297
    for NOOK Color, 13-16
web browsing on NOOK Color, 119-129
    Bookmarks screen, 124-127
    configuring, 127-129
Wi-Fi access
    battery life and
        for NOOK, 170
        for NOOK Color, 5
    enabling/disabling, 176
    hotspot connections
        for NOOK, 169-170
        for NOOK Color, 5-6
    setup for NOOK Color, 3

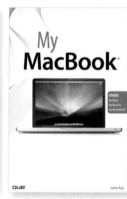

FREE Online Edition

Your purchase of **The NOOK™ Book** includes access to a free online edition for 45 days through the Safari Books Online subscription service. Nearly every Que book is available online through Safari Books Online, along with over 5,000 other technical books and videos from publishers such as Addison-Wesley Professional, Cisco Press, Exam Cram, IBM Press, O'Reilly, Prentice Hall, and Sams.

SAFARI BOOKS ONLINE allows you to search for a specific answer, cut and paste code, download chapters, and stay current with emerging technologies.

Activate your FREE Online Edition at www.informit.com/safarifree

> **STEP 1:** Enter the coupon code: UUBIDDB.

> **STEP 2:** New Safari users, complete the brief registration form. Safari subscribers, just login.

If you have difficulty registering on Safari or accessing the online edition, please e-mail customer-service@safaribooksonline.com